Easy Decorating w...
PAINT &
PAPER

EDITORIAL
Managing Editor: Sheridan Carter
Editorial Coordinator: Margaret Kelly
UK Editorial Consultants: How-To Publications

CONTRIBUTORS
Tonia Todman, pp. 10-17; Virginia Carroll, pp. 18-21; Rod Comish (The Australian Wallpaper Council), pp. 22-35; Jennifer Bennell, pp. 38-47; Andrew Kemp, pp. 48-63; Rob Whelan, pp. 64-77; Verna Simpson, Green Tips

PHOTOGRAPHY
Features Editor: Sandra Hartley
Photographer: Andrew Payne (except where otherwise credited)

PRODUCTION
Tara Barrett
Chris Hatcher

ILLUSTRATIONS
Greg Gaul

COVER
Design: Frank Pithers
Photograph courtesy of VISION

DESIGN AND PRODUCTION MANAGER
Nadia Sbisa

PUBLISHER
Philippa Sandall

Published by J.B. Fairfax Press Pty Ltd
80-82 McLachlan Avenue
Rushcutters Bay 2011
© J.B. Fairfax Press Pty Ltd 1990

EASY DECORATING WITH PAINT & PAPER
Includes Index
ISBN 1 86343 016 4

Formatted by J.B. Fairfax Press Pty Ltd
Output by Adtype, Sydney
Printed by Toppan Printing Co, Hong Kong

Distributed in the UK by
J.B. Fairfax Press Ltd
9 Trinity Centre, Park Farm Estate
Wellingborough, Northants UK
Tel: (0933) 402330
Fax: (0933) 402234

Distributed in Australia by
Newsagents Direct Distributors
and
Storewide Magazine Distributors
150 Bourke Road, Alexandria
NSW 2015

Distributed Internationally by
T.B.Clarke (Overseas) Pty Ltd
80 McLachlan Avenue
Rushcutters Bay NSW 2011
Tel: (02) 360 7566
Fax: (02) 360 7445

New Zealand Agents
Medialine Holdings Ltd
P O Box 100
243 North Shore Mail Centre
Tel: (09) 443 0250
Fax: (09) 443 0249

NOTE TO READERS
This book features many useful skill classes and tips but we cannot anticipate all of your working conditions or the characteristics of your materials and tools. We recommend that for safety reasons you use caution, care and good judgment when following the instructions or procedures in this book. Be aware of your own skill level and the instructions and safety precautions associated with various tools and materials shown. When in doubt always seek professional advice. The publisher cannot assume responsibility for any damage or injury to persons as a result of misuse of the information provided.

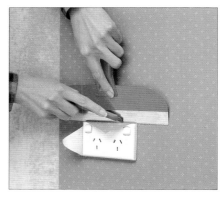

CONTENTS

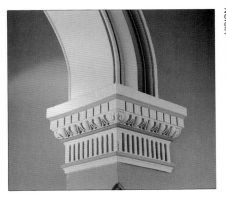

KEY TO SKILL CLASSES

HANGING PREPASTED WALLPAPER

SIMPLE MARBLING

PAINT STRIPPING

READY TO PAINT

INTRODUCTION

*R*oll on the weekend! A time to stop, put your feet up, enjoy a drink, close your eyes and … sink into a deep sleep? Certainly not! It's time to dream up your next home improvement project!

Once you have moved into your home, whether it is brand new and modern, or old and in need of tender loving care, painting and decorating is often the next step. But it doesn't have to create an upheaval in your life or be a major expense. Easy Decorating with Paint & Paper shows you just how easy it can be.

There are loads of Skill Classes, hints and tips – including 'green' ones – to help you make a start. And it really is that easy! There's a section for everyone – from colour scheming, wallcoverings and decorative paint finishes through to interior and exterior painting. Each section is full of practical advice as well as inspiring ideas – the essential tools and equipment you need, safety guidelines, preparation of surfaces, the types of materials you can use to decorate, and lots more – plus over a hundred photographs and illustrations to spur you on!

It's usually best to start at the beginning, so begin with Getting Started (see page 6), and when you are ready, just keep reading!

The weekend is the natural time to undertake projects – after all, most of us only have the weekend to do work around the home. It's amazing what you can achieve, so why not give it a go? Decorating can be a joy and a delight for the home decorator, so let Easy Decorating with Paint & Paper show you the way.

Once you have moved into your home, whether it is brand new and modern or old and in need of tender loving care, painting and decorating is often the next step. Your home should reflect your particular lifestyle and interests, so it is essential – before you begin – to work out what you want and how to achieve it.

GETTING STARTED

There are two important factors to bear in mind with home decorating: the amount of work that has to be done, and how the space you have can best be utilised and enhanced. This applies whether you are planning improvements to an existing home or considering buying a house or an apartment to renovate.

Decorating may cover a multitude of sins – but there are some signs that indicate major problems to be dealt with before you can paint and paper.

❏ Badly stained upper walls – indicates water seepage and is probably caused by a leaking roof. Costly to repair.

❏ Cracks in walls – may be serious or only superficial. Have this checked by a professional.

❏ Badly corroded metal-work and loose or rotting fascia boards – suggests general neglect.

Once you are ready to begin decorating, before you even *look* at colour samples, work out your budget and priority list. Again, this will depend on your lifestyle and special interests – if you are a busy career-minded professional your needs will be very different to those of a family.

Where to start

One way to begin the evaluation process is to make a list of the positive features you like about a room – a colour, a chair, a floor rug? Then make a list of the features you don't like – curtains, wallpaper, a door handle? By becoming more aware of your surroundings you will discover what you like, and begin to define your own sense of style and personal taste. Successful home decorating has a lot to do with understanding your own response to light and space, colour, pattern and texture.

Wall and ceiling surfaces offer as great an opportunity as furnishings to create the mood and character of a room – whatever atmosphere you want is achievable with the right combination of elements. If you don't feel confident, seek professional advice from a design consultant or colour expert (be sure to get a quote for their services first) – the end result will be more than worth it.

If it's a long-term project, walk around with your budget in one hand and your priority list in the other!

❏ **A room-by-room appraisal** may be needed if you are renovating throughout. If you have a specific short-term decorating project in mind then focus your attention on that – but don't

Wallpaper in a child's room with a Paddington Bear theme

forget that each room is part of a larger design scheme.

❏ **Essential tools and equipment.** For the enthusiastic do-it-yourselfer, part of the budget needs to be allocated to buying essential tools and equipment. It pays to remember that more expensive specialist equipment, such as a steam stripper for stripping wallpaper, can be hired. If you are lucky enough, you may have a generous friend or relative who has already made the investment!

Make sure you have all the tools you need before you

start. Don't just make do – good tools and equipment will make all the difference. A very basic set-up would include: a sturdy ladder; drop sheets, newspaper and polythene for covering furniture and floors; stripping and sanding tools; filling knife and filler; a bucket for mixing wallpaper paste, sugar soap, and so on; a paint tray; and a selection of brushes, rollers and cloths.

❏ **Dampness.** Always check for damp before you start decorating. Damp is an insidious problem and if signs of it appear on any walls,

Nairn Decor

TIPSTRIP

TESTING FOR DAMP

Test for damp by placing a piece of aluminium foil over the damp patch. If moisture appears on the foil, condensation is probably the cause. This can be cured by improving the ventilation and insulating to keep the room warm. If the surface stays dry and the back of the foil becomes damp, the moisture may be coming from an outside wall and will need to be treated.

you'll need to treat it first. If damp appears on a top-floor wall, check the roof for leaks; if you discover damp on the ground floor, call in the experts to assess the nature of the problem – you may need to install a damp-proof course (DPC).

❑ **Preparation.** Once you've decided where to start, all the surfaces to be decorated need to be measured and marked up accurately so that you can estimate how much paper and paint you need.

All surfaces to be painted or decorated must be smooth, clean and dry and any cracks filled. Prepare ceilings and floors before woodwork because they create more dust and mess. A room should be decorated in the following order: ceiling, walls and alcoves (if painting), doors, windows, skirtings, walls and alcoves (if wallpapering).

❑ **Test samples.** Before you buy large quantities of paint or wallpaper, get hold of some samples and experiment. Experiment with areas of colour so that you see the changes from natural daylight to artificial light and the changes of light and shade. A small tin of paint or a tiny sampler tin is an excellent investment. Cover the corner of a room and don't worry about the growing number of patches – it's a small price to pay for getting the colour 100

GREEN TIP

Whether you construct things yourself or have them installed, try to avoid using ecologically unsound products.

per cent right! Follow the same approach when choosing a wallpaper – use as large a sample as possible or buy a single roll and look at it in the room under various light conditions.

A question of style

Style is sometimes very hard to define – an informed eye is a real asset when it comes to appreciating what does and doesn't work in a particular room. Look around you – especially at other people's homes. Do you like the decor? How have colour, pattern and texture been used to highlight a surface?

Books and magazines are another source of inspiration, although they usually express current trends. Genuine innovation is important but beware the fickle fashion statement. New fashions come and go, but the classic rule of keeping the background simple always applies.

Another aspect of design is whether or not you feel comfortable with the end result. If you're not happy with it, something isn't right and you might need to think again.

This spacious bathroom uses a combination of tiling, paint and a decorative border with matching curtains to create personality

POINTERS

❑ Budget wisely. Spend most on the things that will receive the greatest wear and tear.

❑ Get the basics right. Pay attention to essential details. Choose simple decoration and colour schemes to provide the right setting, then add personality, excitement and fashion through the things that are easily changed: fabrics, wall colours, rugs, lampshades.

❑ Choose colours with proven staying power so that your decor and accessories gain style and quality with age.

❑ Aim to achieve and preserve a balance of elements in a room.

These tips also apply to the exterior of your home – although here, the need to weatherproof will also determine your choice of materials, colours and textures. Remember too that the larger outdoor setting can be just as important to your home's appearance as architectural style.

The look

The look is all-important – and instantly recognisable when you get it right! A lot of elements go towards creating the look you want – colour scheme, design theme and the room's function, for starters, plus your own personality and lifestyle.

The 'look' is all about creating a pleasant and satisfying environment for the whole family – one that is practical and tailored to meet your needs, and looks good into the bargain.

Aesthetic and practical considerations go hand in hand in creating the look you want. The style, colour and atmosphere of living areas will depend on architectural style, the size and shape of the room, furniture and, again, your lifestyle – how will you be using the room?

Take the kitchen for example: it must be workable, well planned and equipped yet warm, friendly and human.

In bedrooms, the main emphasis is provided by colour and pattern; furniture will also dictate the chosen look. Children's bedrooms

should be designed to change over the years as they develop new hobbies and interests – a soft pastel colour scheme for the nursery can become the bright primaries that small children love so much; teenagers will want something more sophisticated – coordinated wallcoverings and lots of accessories, or a theme design which reflects their latest passion!

In a multipurpose room or one-room living situation, space is always at a premium – keep the look simple and streamlined to maximise that spacious feeling. Here, the look may be created by a neutral or monochromatic colour scheme. You may go for something a little more adventurous, but always remember to choose colour and pattern to suit the purpose of the room.

Laura Ashley

Choose colour and pattern to suit the purpose of the room.

1 This elegant lounge combines muted tones of green and grey with a dramatic, boldly patterned lounge suite

2 This charming, very feminine living room corner has matching wallpaper, curtains and accessories

3 Gentle colours coordinating in matched fabrics bring a restful feeling to this bedroom

Nairn Decor

Dulux

gives it an interesting, highly textured character

6 This fence is a stylish example of composite design combining grey picket fencing with an ornate cream-coloured concrete wall

7 Pattern and texture are beautifully realised in this room

8 This room shows a very soft, green tonal colour scheme and an elegant use of stripes

9 An interesting front door treatment can enhance the entrance to your home

4 This modern, Victorian-style study shows a very clever use of decorative pattern and texture – the unifying factor is the burgundy and beige colour scheme

5 The violet-painted timber facade on this house is both decorative and practical – and

VISION

Wilson

6

5

7

8

9

9

If you've just realised that your home and surroundings are looking a little lacklustre, a stylish colour scheme with the textures of your choice and patterns to suit will work wonders for heart and hearth!

COLOUR SCHEMING

If colour is the magic in a room, texture and pattern help create its character. Conjure up images of some of the rooms you've been in and remembered: bright, festive rooms; warm, friendly rooms; rooms that are stark, cool and modern; or restful one-colour rooms. These images are all created by the colours, patterns and textures used.

Good colour scheming is important for both emotional and economic reasons – apart from the irritation a bad colour choice will cause you, the expense of changing it will be even more upsetting!

Pattern and texture are often secondary considerations to colour when decorating, and sometimes present themselves in subtle, unexpected ways.

Texture is all about the multitude of different surfaces that can be present in a room: the gleam of a silver tray, the velvety leaves of an indoor plant, the ruggedness of a hand-loomed rug, the shine of wall paint or the cool sophistication of marble floors. Even lighting provides texture.

Textural contrast is an essential part of an overall decorating scheme. Too much of any one texture will give a disappointing effect: imagine a room full of shiny chrome furniture and glass, glossy walls, bright lights and a marble floor. Try the balance of velvet or silverware with shiny wood, leather furniture with hand-woven cushions and rugs, pine with contemporary fabric prints or a floral-patterned wallpaper with a plain cotton fabric.

Patterns, whether bold and beautiful or tiny and discreet, set the design and style of any room. Scale is the vital element to consider when choosing patterns. Put simply, big and small patterns each work in very different ways. Some simple rules may help:

❑ A one-colour paint, fabric and paper scheme will make for a spacious effect in any room or hallway.

❑ Large rooms that are generally well lit can be broadly decorated with bold patterns. Walls, floors and soft furnishings can all be treated lavishly with the same or related patterns.

❑ Small rooms ideally suit small-scaled patterns. By using a selection of related small prints in your soft furnishings, wallpapers and accessories a feeling of greater spaciousness will emerge.

❑ A small amount of large-scaled pattern goes a long way in a small room. Complement, or 'tie together' this burst of pattern with coordinating or related colours and small-print fabrics.

Remember, before you decide on the colour scheme for a particular room, put together a sample board showing all of the different colours, textures and patterns you are planning to use in the room – this will include the room's 'givens', for example, carpet and soft furnishings.

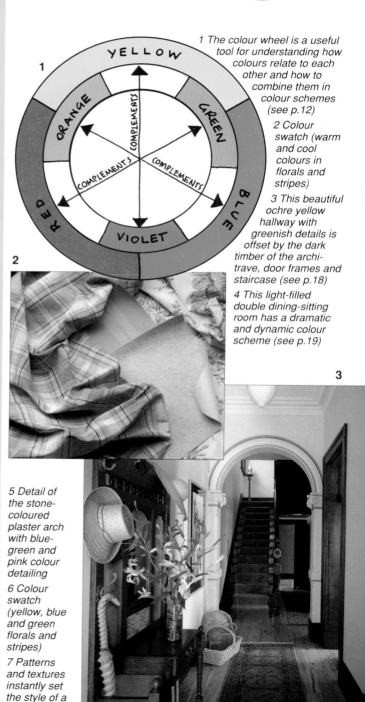

1 The colour wheel is a useful tool for understanding how colours relate to each other and how to combine them in colour schemes (see p.12)

2 Colour swatch (warm and cool colours in florals and stripes)

3 This beautiful ochre yellow hallway with greenish details is offset by the dark timber of the architrave, door frames and staircase (see p.18)

4 This light-filled double dining-sitting room has a dramatic and dynamic colour scheme (see p.19)

5 Detail of the stone-coloured plaster arch with blue-green and pink colour detailing

6 Colour swatch (yellow, blue and green florals and stripes)

7 Patterns and textures instantly set the style of a room (see pp.16-17)

4

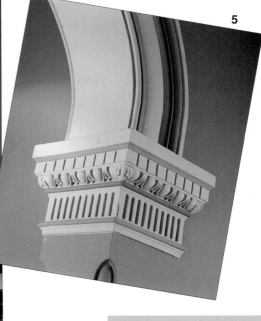

5

Colour is one of the most useful of all the tools at the decorator's disposal – it can make a small room seem larger, a dark room lighter, or completely change the whole mood of a room.

6

7

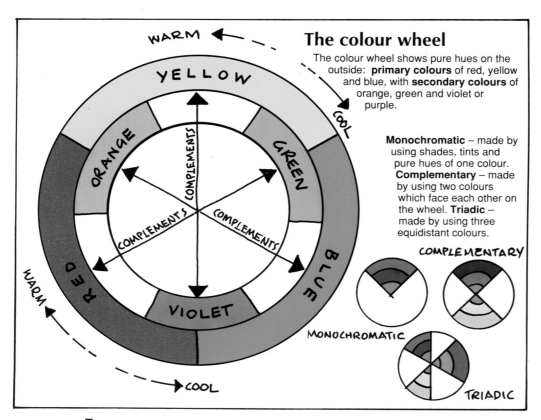

The colour wheel

The colour wheel shows pure hues on the outside: **primary colours** of red, yellow and blue, with **secondary colours** of orange, green and violet or purple.

Monochromatic – made by using shades, tints and pure hues of one colour. **Complementary** – made by using two colours which face each other on the wheel. **Triadic** – made by using three equidistant colours.

All fabrics and wallpapers are designed by experts, so why not cheat a little? Pick out the colours from your favourite design and match them with paint and accessories.

Cool colours are 'receding' and appear to be going away from you. Cool colours – greens, blue-greens and blues – are useful for creating spaciousness, and a cool, calm, more impersonal atmosphere.

If you choose to use equal quantities of a cool and a warm colour in a room, the warm colour will always dominate.

Black and white are theoretically non-colours and are excellent for adding emphasis and impact.

Colour schemes

First consider your room's basic features. Analyse its shape, size, ceiling height, doorways and aspect. How much natural light does it get? Do you need to help it along with extra light fittings?

Colour can be most effective in changing the shape of a room. A very high ceiling can appear to be lower if you paint it with a dark, rich colour – especially if you then paint the floor to match, or carpet in a similar colour.

Colour swatch

Colour

Remember, one colour does not cost any more than another.

Whether you're creating a brand new colour scheme or updating an existing one, it's important to plan it properly. Spend some time on it – look at other people's colour schemes and make a note of colour combinations you find pleasing. Work out what kind of look you want. Think of which colours convey the right mood. A well-thought-out colour scheme will greatly enhance your living environment.

The colour wheel

The colour wheel is a useful tool for understanding how colours relate to each other and how to combine them in colour schemes. To success-fully work with colour and

make correct choices, you need to understand how the wheel works.

On the outside of the wheel are the three primary colours: red, blue and yellow. These are pure colours. By mixing two primary colours together you achieve a secondary colour: green from blue and yellow, orange from red and yellow, and violet from red and blue. These six colours make up the basic colour spectrum. The colours which appear opposite each other on the wheel (blue opposite orange, red opposite green, and yellow opposite violet) are called complemen-tary pairs and they offer the greatest possible contrast between colours, since the secondary colour contains no trace of its complementary.

Warm and cool

The colour wheel is divided into warm and cool colours. The half containing yellow, orange and red is warm, while the remaining half – containing violet, blue and

green – is cool.

Warm colours are regarded as 'advancing' or dominant, as they appear to advance towards you and can create an enclosing, warm and intimate feeling.

When planning a warm scheme, remember that the closer the colour is to a warm primary (red or yellow), the stronger it is. Large areas of these colours are hard to live with, so choose their softer cousins such as pink or peach, reserving the stronger colours for accents only.

Vertical stripes will appear to raise the ceiling height, while horizontal bands of colour, perhaps below a chair rail, or as a wide wallpaper border, will appear to lower it. A long narrow room will appear squarer if the opposite narrow ends are painted in a strong colour, with the other two walls in a lighter colour.

❑ If your room is cold and receives no sunshine, choose from the range of warm colours – whether they be dark or light, rich and strong or pale and soft.

Dark, cold rooms need sunshine! Don't worry if it doesn't pour through the windows, create the feeling by using warm oranges, yellows, rich creams contrasted with glistening white or ivory.

❑ If the room is small and cramped, use pastel colours like peach, cream, beige and yellow – but keep them warm and welcoming.

Warm, well-lit rooms can take on an elegant look with cool greens, lilacs, pale yellows, pale grey and black and white. Judge whether the size of your room demands strong or paler shades, and what volume of these colours will be successful.

A colour is affected by everything else around it – especially light and shadow, as well as other colours. Light affects the tone, warmth and clarity of colour.

Harmonious colour schemes
A harmonious colour scheme uses colours which are closely related on the colour wheel – blue and green, for example – leading to a comfortable, uniform blend of colours throughout the room or house. Harmonious groups of colours include pink, apricot, peach and gold, or clear

Chickens and roosters wallpaper – a modern kitchen with a white, grey and red colour scheme

blues, blue-green, aqua and green. In harmonious schemes, nothing clashes or overwhelms and there is a sense of continuity and flow. This is generally an 'easy-to-live-with' scheme with a relaxed feeling. Harmonious schemes provide a good background for patterned furnishing fabrics as they will not compete.

A lounge room with a neutral colour scheme – beige with natural timber furniture

---

POINTERS
❑ *Colours look different in different types of light.* Make sure you try out a large sample of the colour in the room where it will be used.
❑ *A colour affects the colours next to it.* Bear this in mind before putting your favourite shade of pink next to a certain green that screams at it!
❑ *The amount of colour used affects how you see it.* An entire room of deep purple may be hard to live with, but small amounts of it in a mushroom-beige room may work like a charm.

Muted green and white hallway with stained timber floor

Dulux

Colour codes

Each colour has basic characteristics representing associations and various moods. Everyone responds to colour in their own way. It is interesting to look at a range of colours and examine their different qualities.

Red ranges from the intense colour that symbolises vitality and aggressiveness, to the romantic roses and pastel pinks that have never been out of favour. It is the strongest advancing colour, it can make you feel physically warm, and it is also appetite-inducing – hence the many restaurants decorated in reds. Rose and pink shades are eternally regarded as feminine, delicate and romantic! Deeper tones of red – the plums and burgundys – can impart an elegant, traditional feel, and look wonderful in large rooms in old houses, and hallways.

Orange is said to have the physical energy of red, with the intellectual associations of yellow. It works well in a stimulating scheme if contrasted with a neutral or complementary colour, and is a good contender for bright busy rooms for children. Orange lightens to the favoured peaches and apricots which can be ideal bedroom colours, for they appear to be neither masculine or feminine in the extreme. Orange darkens to wonderful terracottas, tans and browns. These become masculine, warm and relaxed.

Green is the refreshing colour of nature, and brings the outdoors inside – which could be important if you live in a multi-floored apartment building! Green in every shade works well with

contrasts. Take care if using artificial light with green as it is prone to unexpected tonal changes. Be sure you check your colour swatch under all the different lighting possibilities in your room before proceeding.

Yellow is one of the more complex colours. It can be joyful, intellectual, strong and stimulating in all the various tones and is certainly one of the best colours for bringing light and warmth into a cold, dull room. Pale yellows are a good choice for hallways, as they are highly reflective, but take care to put lots of neutrals or white with yellows or they can become over-whelming. Darker shades of yellow are rich and elegant, but be cautious with yellow-greens as they can dull to grey in artificial or dull light.

Choosing colours is exciting – but with so many possibilities to choose from it's hard to know where to start. That's where samples come in – collect a variety of different samples for a successful colour scheme

Monochromatic colour schemes

'Monochrome' describes a scheme in shades of one colour plus white (or some-times black). This kind of colour scheme is sometimes referred to as 'tone-on-tone'. Take care to emphasise differing textures in this scheme, as without these contrasts the scheme can become very flat.

Contrast colour schemes

A contrast scheme brings together 'complementaries' – colours that are directly opposite each other on the wheel. Contrast schemes can be used to brighten up a room; used close together complementaries intensify each other, creating a lively and stimulating decor.

Neutral colours

Most colour schemes benefit from the introduction of neutral colours. Neutrals range from white through to creams, beiges, tans and browns, and from pale silvery

grey through to black. They are useful for combining with more definite colours and can also be used to create all-neutral schemes. Textures also play a part in any neutral scheme by adding variety and interest.

Accent colours

Most colour schemes, especially ones based on neutral colours, benefit from the addition of an accent or highlight colour. Accents add the finishing touches to an overall scheme.

Tones

Tone describes the lightness or darkness of a colour. Think of a black-and-white photograph where colours have been converted into black, white and grey. Now imagine a room decorated entirely in light-toned colours – it would photograph as the same shade of grey! By using a range of tones – whatever the colours – a colour scheme becomes richer and more satisfying.

GIRL'S BEDROOM AND GUEST ROOM

This bedroom receives lots of light all day long. A delicate and cheerful pale orange and peach colour scheme was chosen – delightfully reflected in the full-length extravaganza of curtains.

Other 'givens' here were the low ceiling and white ceiling fan, the exposed stained timber beams and skirting boards.

This room will eventually become a guest room – the amount of available light means that it could easily support a much stronger colour scheme if desired at a later stage.

GREEN TIP
Interior colour schemes make the most of natural light if they are pale and warm. Pale tones will reflect light and make spaces look bigger.

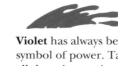

Violet has always been the symbol of power. Take note of all the aristocratic and religious robes coloured thus! Interestingly, violet in its stronger shades can be seen as either cool or warm: red-violet can work in the same way as reds and pinks, blue-violet has similar characteristics to blue. Paler shades of violet too will move between warm and cold depending on the quantities of red or blue the shade contains. Lilac is thought of as romantic, or sometimes as a colour of mourning – so your choice is definitely a question of attitude! It is the shade of some of the most loved flowers, and a particularly flattering colour in its softer pink shades.

Blue is probably the most universally acceptable colour for any situation. Traditional blue and white is still enormously popular, and appears together on fabric, wallpaper and crockery. Light blue will bring the skies inside and instil a calming atmosphere into any room. It is not a reflective colour in its medium to dark shades, so take note of this if planning to paint a small room; or use this to your advantage if painting a bright sunroom or conservatory. Lighter shades will certainly expand any area but, as with yellow, blue needs the contrast of neutrals or white to offset it.

Pastels, made by lightening pure colour with lots of white, are soft, gentle colours which always blend well with both modern and traditional styles of furnishings. Any pastel colour will coordinate with another, even opposites on the colour wheel.

Contrasting colours in a room can be strong and visually stunning, or gently coloured and restful. Remember, the less intense the shades you choose, the easier the scheme will become.

Pattern and texture

The secret of successful decorating is a simple one – contrasting textures and patterns bring any scheme to life by creating interest and the mood of a room.

Nothing could be worse than to spend valuable time carefully working out your colour scheme, combining fabrics with paints and papers, to find that the whole thing looks flat and somehow wrong.

Patterns and textures instantly set the style of a room. They behave in a similar way to colours – small, pale-coloured patterns recede, creating a spacious feeling, whereas bold patterns in bright colours advance and will make the room appear smaller.

Texture can create style sometimes just as easily as patterns. This will depend on your choice of certain traditional fabric weaves – calico or homespun, coarse hand-loomed rugs, sheer muslins, laces, velvets and silks, wools and embroidered tapestries. All these fabrics instantly create a well-recognised style.

Scale, as we have discussed earlier, is a vital consideration when choosing patterns. This element is really easy to decide, and is governed by the size of your room and its main architectural features – ceiling height, number of doorways, size and height of windows and other features, such as a fireplace or built-in shelves. Large-scale patterns do not work well if they are cut into often or in uneven ways, which eliminates matching. For example, matching a large-print wallpaper in a room which has wall interruptions of fireplace, shelving, two doors and large, different-sized windows would be difficult. The pattern would start and finish at odd spots, and could create disturbing optical illusions. Large-scaled fabric on a small chair could overwhelm the chair, and not really do the print justice.

Small rooms can easily be overtaken by large patterns and bold colours used to excess. Large patterns are most suited to large rooms, where they can be used generously and displayed with creative style. Small areas of large patterns in small rooms *can* be most effective, but you must take care to balance its scale with smaller, related prints and textures in coordinating colours.

TIPSTRIP

MIX LIKE WITH LIKE
Select patterns and colours which relate to one another in some way. Many manufacturers make this easy for you by producing whole ranges of fabrics that are related. Coordination does not necessarily mean to match – it means that you can mix together fabrics that have common elements of design and colour. This mixing together of related prints and colours can give a room a surprisingly spacious and pleasant aspect. It's really much easier than it looks!

Large rooms can take large patterns on most surfaces. Walls can be papered or painted with strong colours or patterns and even a patterned carpet could be just right. Small patterns on walls can seem to glow more than a plain surface, though this will depend on the colours used in the pattern. The key to

using scale correctly is to develop an eye for balance. Don't use too much of any one colour or pattern unless it seems perfectly correct to, and make all your decisions with the size and proportion of your room in mind. As your eye develops this skill, you will feel more confident about using patterns and colours that are out of the ordinary. Until you can do this with ease, either accept professional advice or tread a conservative path.

There are some easy categories to remember when choosing style, most of which have established patterns with complementary textures to choose from.

❏ **Traditional** includes a variety of styles from history, such as Victorian, Edwardian, Art Deco, Classical and Georgian. Wallpapers and furniture abound in these styles, most of which are easily duplicated today with reproduction furniture and fabrics to suit. Colour in these

styles is a personal choice, though the style of furniture chosen usually dictates suitable colour and pattern size.

❏ **Florals** are probably the most flexible of patterns and fit into almost all styles. They can be large or small, formal or informal, traditional or contemporary. Worked with stripes they become formal; when shown in bright primaries as crayoned drawings they can appear very casual. Large abstract prints are very contemporary and tiny prints are definitely country-style in character.

❏ **Neutrals** can form a valuable link between two opposing patterns. Simply choose a small print in a colour common to both patterns and you will tie the three pattern areas together. They can be overwhelming if used in large quantities, but are useful in delightfully bridging gaps.

❏ **Ethnic patterns** are trad-

itional patterns which come from all over the world and have become classics.

These rich and diverse patterns and textures can create stylish casual atmospheres independently, or work well when combined in small quantities with other styles.

Batik fabric, Mexican pottery and hand-woven fabrics, primitive statues, Indian hand-print fabrics and Oriental silks are all instantly recognisable for their inherent style and have a feeling of timelessness about them.

❏ **Geometrics and abstracts** are similar to neutrals, but have a more classical approach to design. These patterns are suitable for contemporary home decor, and can be as diverse as an all-over two-colour geometric pattern, or fabrics printed with photographed texture simulating painting techniques.

Metallic fabric surfaces work well in this style, as do fabrics with interesting

TIPSTRIP

PAINT AND PAPER
Wallpapers and paints have textures that can quickly and economically bring a different look to the room. The range of wallpapers today is astonishing — from glittery metal foils through to traditional velvet flocks, to hand-woven hessian, linen and silk effects and even simulated bricks and ceramic tiles. Apart from observing some pointers about caring for the surface of the material, most of these wallcoverings can be easily installed by the home handyperson.

Decorative paint techniques can create subtle textures — try sponging and stippling for wall effects. Even the use of full-gloss paint on all woodwork can introduce a new texture.

surface textures — either lustrous, coarse, open-weave or embroidered.

Pattern and texture are essential ingredients in any room scheme

Colour stories

Every room in a house has its unique colour story – but it is also part of a whole. This house was chosen for its stylish architectural features and the way colour has been used to bring them to life.

Hallway

This beautiful hallway has no natural light source or direct sunlight except for that from the front door and the stained-glass window halfway up the staircase – so the aim was to give it a cheerful, sunny feeling. A strong deep ochre yellow with greenish details was chosen to work against the dark timber of the architrave, door frames and staircase. The yellow is made warmer by being reflected in the highly polished golden-orange timber floor – the reflectiveness of the floor and the pale green-grey ceiling together make the most of the available natural light.

Colour here was also used as a means of articulating a quite long rambling house: beginning at the front door one looks down the hallway through yellow to a strong blueish red at the end. The various 'locks', and twists and turns off the hallway are also red and act like punctuation points in the overall scheme.

The yellow and red combination is offset by the muted green detailing on the architrave. This kind of colour detailing is a recurring design feature (see the blue-green and pink detailing on the architrave in the dining-sitting room) – because the hallway has so many rooms off it, this was one way to create a sense of continuity or relationship from one room to the next.

Double dining-sitting room

This beautiful combination double dining-sitting room faces sunlight all day. The two reflective surfaces of highly polished floor and stone-coloured ceiling also serve to increase the light level in the room. The French doors were added to open out the room even more.

The amount of light and stained woodwork in the room meant that this dramatic cool blue-green colour could be chosen for the walls. The colour complements and enhances the woodwork and beautiful wooden furniture, and interacts with the warm, golden-orange timber floor. The wall colour vibrates against and is complemented by the colour of the floor next to it. This dynamic colour equation is also reinforced by the gold, orange and green accents in the stained glass window and fireplace surround.

Architrave (detail)

This charming stone-coloured plaster arch is colour-linked to the ceiling and is a stunning feature of the room. The subtle colour detailing is designed to 'recede' rather than compete or overwhelm. The blue-green detail has been painted a lighter tone than that used for the walls and the pink detail was taken from the orient-inspired painting on the left of the room.

In contrast to this kind of detailing, the ornate centrepiece on the ceiling is moulded by light rather than colour.

Don't overdo colour details or have big tonal jumps on architectural features like architraves, door frames and picture rails.

Breakfast room

This light-filled breakfast room is an extension of the kitchen and is essentially a garden room – the French doors open out onto a terracotta tile patio and a lush garden full of trees.

A neutral colour scheme (number 4 in a tonal range of 1-10) was chosen for this room for several reasons. On the one hand, a quiet, peaceful atmosphere was required; on the other hand, the room had two dominant givens – lots of strong woodwork and the dominant surface texture of a red and grey granite worktop.

A heavy dark green-grey laminate was chosen for the cupboards and a neutral khaki green-grey colour for the walls. One enters this room through the red 'lock' at the end of the yellow hallway.

Blue and white bedroom

This bedroom receives lots of warm light – perfect for this strong, fresh icy Wedgwood blue and white colour scheme.

The important givens here were the white iron bed, the pale white and grey-veined Carrara marble fireplace, the stained wood skirting boards and the silvery burgundy carpet.

When choosing a new wall colour, consider the room's aspect and amount of light, architectural qualities, scale, purpose and existing features – for example, woodwork (light or dark, painted or stained), carpet, soft furnishings, and so on.

20

Master bedroom

Two important givens influenced the colour scheme selected for this room (above right): the silvery burgundy carpet and the enormous amount of light from the windows (not pictured). The room's crowning glory is the beautiful hand-painted frieze. The colours are made up of a strong red, aqua green and a stronger green. A stippling brush was used in parts to deliberately 'fade back' some colours.

Although this room has a lot of light and could have handled a much stronger colour scheme, a light, quiet feeling was wanted. Instead of the light, warm colours coming forward and the dark, cool colours receding, in this instance tone overwhelms everything else to create a quietly dramatic effect.

The pale grey of the painted woodwork, the

If you can't work out what is missing from a colour scheme – it's often the tonal mix that is wrong.

mushroom-coloured walls and white ceiling are offset by the solid warmth of the frieze and, behind the bed, the dark red tone of the recessed arch (again referring back to the red 'lock' colour in the hallway). The arch is, in fact, quite shallow but the dark tone gives it more depth – making it hard to tell where the surface starts and finishes. The brass bed adds a glossy warm dimension of colour and texture to the overall scheme.

Few do-it-yourself activities in the home provide more satisfaction than wallpapering. And if you are already saying to yourself, 'Oh, it's too hard for me', think again.

WALLCOVERINGS

These days the new-generation vinyl-based wallpapers (which come prepasted and virtually ready to put straight on the wall) are very forgiving and make paperhanging so easy for first-timers.

With wallpaper the rewards are rapid and dramatic in the sudden transformation of a tired bedroom, a bland lounge or a problem hallway. What's more, the wallpaper comes off the wall as easily as it went on, so you are not locked forever into a certain look or style. And when you do eventually redecorate, there are no big headaches and no mess!

Use wallpaper, and that includes borders, to inject life, colour and style into the gloomiest of rooms. Create a feeling of coolness in a room that gets a lot of warm light and add warmth and cosiness to rooms in the house that get little or no sunlight.

Echo your lifestyle and individual sense of design in the wallpapers you choose – and what a choice! Whether you are seeking a city-smart look for a townhouse or a country cottage look for a terrace, there's a huge range of superb designs to cater for your taste.

Choose a wallpaper pattern to create the atmosphere and style you want – the number of patterns available is enormous. Wallcoverings can also be used to cover up a multitude of sins, for example, all-over prints can help to disguise odd corners, awkward angles and uneven wall surfaces.

Coordinating fabrics help to give a unified feel.

With wallpapering, as in most DIY activities, the golden rule is to take your time and enjoy the activity. That means spending a little extra time in preparation and not rushing the wallpapering itself. And don't put pressure on yourself either – that's important. Try to do a good job without seeking perfection, especially if it's your first attempt.

Preparing your walls for wallpapering is an important stage and most of the wall types you'll encounter are described in this section.

You'll also find a complete list of the tools required. When you do a check you'll probably find that you already have many of the items at home, such as a sponge, a pair of scissors, a pencil and so on.

Calculating how much wallpaper you'll need no longer requires the skill of a mathematician! There's a handy ready reckoner on page 27 which you can use for walls and ceilings.

Most wallpaper retailers are funds of information, so don't hesitate to use them as a resource – not only for your wallpaper but also for solutions to any questions you have about your particular project.

With today's wallpapers you can be bold and adventurous, or careful and conservative. It's up to you. One thing is certain – when you do wallpaper, you'll have lots of fun!

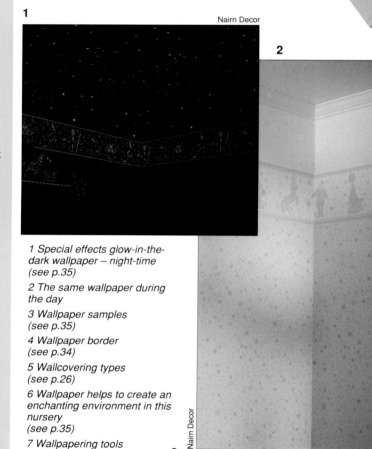

Nairn Decor

1 Special effects glow-in-the-dark wallpaper – night-time (see p.35)

2 The same wallpaper during the day

3 Wallpaper samples (see p.35)

4 Wallpaper border (see p.34)

5 Wallcovering types (see p.26)

6 Wallpaper helps to create an enchanting environment in this nursery (see p.35)

7 Wallpapering tools

Nairn Decor

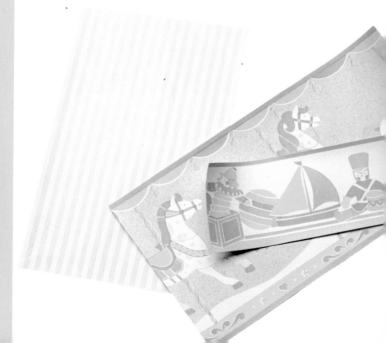

4

5

GREEN TIP

VINYL WALLCOVERINGS
Working from the floor up-wards, use a mild, biode-gradable washing-up liquid solution on small areas at a time; rinse and dry before working on the next bit.

6

Nairn Decor

The number of patterns available in wallcoverings is enormous, ranging from colourful spatter designs and formal florals, to simple geometrics. Choose the perfect pattern for your room.

7

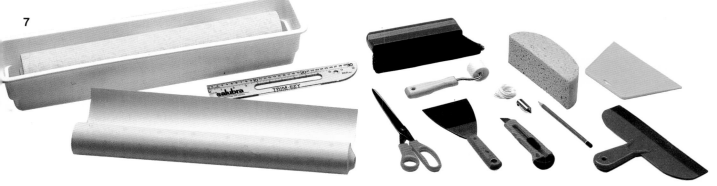

Tools for the job

It's surprising how many of the tools you'll need to hang wallpaper are to be found around the house.

There are some specialist items, however, which make the project easier and successful and are available at your wallpaper store. Before you start you'll need:

❏ a sponge to remove surplus paste and moisture
❏ a pencil to mark on the wall where you will hang your strips
❏ a straightedge to use when trimming surplus paper
❏ a trimming knife
❏ scissors to cut your strips (a long-blade pair is best)
❏ a ruler
❏ a plumb line for obtaining true verticals to align your wallpaper – few rooms are square
❏ a plastic smoother to flatten wallpaper onto walls
❏ a lay brush – this has stiff bristles to press wallpaper into place and is usually used for embossed wallpaper
❏ a seam roller to smooth edges and joins – don't use with embossed wallpaper
❏ a water trough for pre-pasted wallpaper in which you immerse the cut rolled strip prior to hanging
❏ wall size to provide a suitable working surface – always apply size the day before wallpapering
❏ a stepladder to reach the high spots
❏ a table or bench on which to work
❏ sandpaper for smoothing and preparing walls

Wallpapering terms

Anti-fungicide: A solution applied to walls where mildew or mould is a problem. Anti-fungicide has a fairly short life. If you need to treat your walls be sure to start wallpapering soon after.
Bolt: A roll of wallpaper as it's supplied by the manufacturer. A standard bolt or roll is 10.05 m long and 520 mm wide.
Batch number: A number stamped on every roll which indicates the batch or printing job lot. Because printing processes may vary, it's important to make sure all the rolls you buy carry the same batch number.
Borders: Narrow strips of wallpaper easy to apply and with unlimited decorative possibilities.
Bubbles: These are often caused by paste and sometimes appear beneath the wallpaper immediately after it has been hung. They usually dry out. If the bubble is trapped air, use a syringe to inject paste beneath the paper then smooth out.
Butt joints: Strips of wallpaper matched and hung alongside each other edge to edge so the joins don't overlap.
Companions: Different wallcoverings designed and coloured to relate to each other.
Cornice: Usually a plaster moulding separating walls from ceiling.
Dado: The lower part of the wall, often to chair height, which may be defined by a moulding or border.
Drop pattern: A wallpaper pattern which repeats itself diagonally.
Embossed paper: Sometimes known as Duplex, this is wallpaper with a raised pattern or relief effect. Don't use a roller when smoothing or you risk flattening the embossing!
Fixtures: Refers to lights, switch plates and other permanent items attached to walls which wallpaper will be cut around.
Florals: Wallpapers with designs consisting mainly of flowers and foliage.
Frieze: See Borders.
Glue size: Applied to walls before papering, it allows you to move or 'slip' the wallpaper into position and creates better adhesion.
Lining paper: Plain wallpaper used as a base to provide a smooth surface for paper hanging, especially on uneven and cement-rendered walls.
Machine printing: Most wallpapers today are manufactured on a rotary type printing press which produces consistent and clear patterns.
Matching: Hanging strips of paper so the pattern will be in correct relation to the previous strip. There are several types of matching. *Random matching* will look well no matter how one panel is placed in relation to the previous. Stripes, all-over textures and grasscloth patterns can all be randomly matched. *Straight match* is where the pattern on one strip must be joined with a

pattern across the wall. *Drop matching* has a portion of the pattern on each strip like the straight match. However, the pattern will not repeat itself at the same distance from the ceiling line when the wall is finished. Instead, the matching point drops lower with each succeeding strip.

Paste: Adhesive used to attach wallpaper to walls. Most common are cellulose and starch.

Pattern: The design on wallpaper which is repeated throughout the roll.

Peelable wallpaper: Wallpaper with a vinyl layer that allows it to be peeled off the wall without scraping. It leaves a thin layer of paper which can easily be removed or retained, if sound, as a clean surface on which to redecorate.

Plumb line: Weight attached to a length of string and used to obtain the perpendicular for accurate paper hanging.

Pretrimmed wallpaper: Wallpaper from which the manufacturer has trimmed the edges.

Prepasted wallpaper: Most wallpaper today has a film of dry paste on the back which only requires wetting to soften and gain adhesion.

Preparation: Preparing the wall or ceiling prior to hanging. An important step in paper hanging which may involve sanding down and sizing the surface.

Roll: See Batch number.

Scrubbable wallpaper: Vinyl (polyvinyl chloride or PVC) wallpapers are usually scrubbable and can be cleaned using soap or detergent and a soft bristle brush. Be careful not to scrub across seams.

Seams: There are several methods of joining seams. The butt joint in which the edges fit tightly together produces the smoother effect and is the most popular because it leaves a flat, invisible seam.

Sealer: A liquid used to seal porous surfaces such as plasterboard and plaster which might otherwise leach moisture from the paste and prevent adhesion.

Shading: See Batch number.

Size: See Glue size.

Slip: The ability of wallpaper to be moved and patterns matched when in contact with the wall surface. The application of glue size to the wall before commencing papering further assists slip.

Straightedge: A ruler used to give a clean and consistent edge when cutting or trimming wallpaper.

Straight match: Patterned wallpaper where the design is such that the matching points on either side of a strip are opposite each other.

Strippable wallpaper: Wallpaper that can be completely removed without scraping.

Substrate: The backing of wallpaper which is laminated to the design layer.

Sugar soap: Coarse abrasive soap used to clean, degrease and prepare walls for paper hanging.

Vinyl: A range of durable wallpapers which include flexible film, resin and plastic coating.

Water trough: The shallow box used when hanging prepasted wallpaper.

INTERNATIONAL WALLPAPER SYMBOLS

PREPASTED	SCRUBBABLE	DRY PEELABLE
EXCELLENT LIGHTFAST (6-7)	LIGHTFASTNESS (4-5)	FULLY TRIMMED INDIVIDUALLY PACKED
FREE MATCH	STRAIGHT MATCH	OFFSET MATCH
LOW WASHABLE	MEDIUM WASHABLE	HIGH WASHABLE

1 Water trough
2 Rule and trim edge
3 Lay brush
4 Wallpaper shears
5 Seam roller
6 Stripping knife
7 Plumb bob
8 Craft knife
9 Pencil for marking verticals
10 Sponge
11 Plastic smoother
12 Broad knife
13 Steam stripper

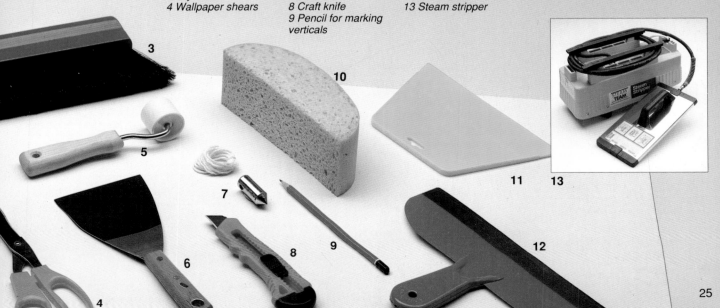

Types of wallcovering

Perhaps the most difficult task you'll face when you decide to wallpaper is choosing the type of wallcovering. The range is quite amazing and sourced from all over the world.

Main types

❑ **Lining paper:** An inexpensive neutral-coloured wallpaper used to cover uneven walls. Decorative wallpaper (or paint) is applied over the lining.

❑ **Vinyl:** Vinyl accounts for a large percentage of today's wallpaper sales. Made from polyvinyl chloride (PVC) it is a highly flexible, serviceable material which is resistant to water and can be scrubbed with a soft bristle brush to remove most marks. It is usually prepasted.

❑ **Vinyl coating:** Liquid PVC is applied to wallpaper giving a more durable, washable surface than paper.

❑ **Embossed vinyl:** PVC moulded to give a raised pattern and backed by a tough paper substrate.

❑ **Blown vinyl:** A relief design effect created by expanding vinyl during manufacture.

❑ **Duplex:** Two sheets of paper bonded to give the wallpaper strength. It can be sponged but not scrubbed.

❑ **Naturals:** Grasscloth and silks, cork, wood veneers, hessian are all made from natural materials applied to paper backings. Hanging them usually requires some degree of experience so they are not recommended for a first-time DIY project.

❑ **Flock:** Flock wallcoverings are regarded as an elegant background for traditional decor and furnishings. Finely chopped wool, rayon or nylon is applied to the design, which is coated with adhesive. The result is a luxurious velvet effect.

❑ **Relief papers:** Usually white and not to be confused with the embossed vinyls or flocks, relief papers include anaglypta, which was a great favourite in Victorian times. Anaglypta is made by bonding two sheets of paper then passing it through deeply embossed rollers.

❑ **Mylar:** This is a new type of foil and is made from tough polymeric polyester which is a resin that becomes a flexible plastic sheet. It looks like real foil but won't show creases after hanging.

❑ **Foil:** A thin, flexible metal sheet – often aluminium – is laminated to a substrate of paper or fabric. The result is an exotic wallcovering with excellent reflective qualities. Use it for accent areas such as one wall of a bathroom or in a hallway.

❑ **Murals:** Usually produced in sets of panels, they range from maps of the world to scenes of autumnal forests and tropical islands. They can cover an entire wall and are excellent to create a feeling of spaciousness in small rooms, especially those without windows.

Charming lounge corner with striped wallpaper and ducks and drakes border

Special wallcoverings

Fabric wallcoverings and other exotic or delicate types such as flock and grasscloth mean special care is required when preparing and hanging. Try at all times to keep paste off the surface. Your wallpaper retailer will be able to suggest the correct paste to use. In the case of fabrics you usually paste the wall first.

How many rolls?

It's easy to calculate the number of rolls you'll need to complete a room. Measure the distance from the floor or skirting board to the ceiling; next, measure the total distance around the room, taking into account doors and windows.

Using the guide below you can see how much wallpaper to buy. For example, if your wall height is between 2.1 and 2.2 m and the distance around the room is about 8.5 m, you'll need five rolls.

Remember the average bolt or roll measures 10.05 m x 530 mm and the chart is scaled to this size. Some of the more exotic wallcoverings such as silk and cork may have different dimensions – ask your wallpaper retailer to work out the quantity using your room measurements.

Walls		Distance around the room (doors and windows included)																		
METRES		8.53	9.75	10.97	12.19	13.41	14.63	15.85	17.07	18.29	19.51	20.73	21.95	23.16	24.38	25.60	26.82	28.04	29.26
	FEET	28'	32'	36'	40'	44'	48'	52'	56'	60'	64'	68'	72'	76'	80'	84'	88'	92'	96'
2.13 to 2.29	6' 10" to 7' 6"	5	5	6	6	7	7	8	8	9	9	10	10	10	11	11	13	13	14
2.30 to 2.44	7' 7" to 8' 0"	5	5	6	6	7	7	8	9	9	10	10	11	11	12	13	14	14	15
2.45 to 2.59	8' 1" to 8' 6"	5	6	6	7	7	8	8	9	9	10	10	12	12	13	14	15	15	15
2.60 to 2.74	8' 7" to 9' 0"	5	6	6	7	7	8	9	9	10	10	11	13	13	14	14	15	15	16
2.75 to 2.90	9' 1" to 9' 6"	5	6	7	7	8	8	9	10	10	11	11	13	14	14	15	15	16	17
2.91 to 3.05	9' 7" to 10' 0"	6	6	7	8	8	9	10	10	11	11	12	14	14	15	16	16	17	17
3.06 to 3.20	10' 1" to 11' 6"	6	6	7	8	9	9	10	11	11	12	13	14	15	16	16	17	18	18
Number of rolls required																			

Shopping checklist

Because most of their business is DIY, wallpaper retailers can be a fund of information and help. You can purchase everything you'll need, from the wallpaper to the tools.

Most shops carry large 'libraries' of pattern books which carry entire ranges in a variety of different patterns and colours. The wallpaper manufacturers supply the books and take much of the guesswork and risk out of decorating by including thoughtfully coordinated ranges; that is, wallpaper teamed with matching borders and fabrics.

However, you don't want to spend hours wading through sample books. This usually leads to confusion and frustration! Instead, when you visit your local supplier, take a checklist containing some basic information so you get the best advice and guidance.

Make a note of the rooms to be decorated. This includes their size; colour and style of the curtains, carpets and other furnishings; the direction windows face; and the colours of adjoining rooms.

Let's say it's the dining room you are going to wallpaper. The furnishings in most dining rooms consist of table, chairs, perhaps a sideboard and china cabinet. These add up to a mass of hard textures, so the decorating solution is to soften walls visually with the use of wallpaper.

A good retailer will be able to show you an imaginative range of options; and don't be afraid to select something that reflects your personality and individuality. Try one of the superb flocks – brilliant if you're lucky enough to have a chandelier.

You might prefer a grasscloth – real or imitation – with its horizontal weave and texture, which creates the illusion of the room being larger than it really is.

Damask design wallpaper creates a tapestry effect and is the perfect companion to period furniture.

Floral designs go with any style of furniture and there's an astonishing range from which to choose. Tiny cottage-type floral prints are perfect for a small dining room, while the large bold florals provide a dramatic backdrop for a larger room.

Still not sure? As well as pattern books, many retailers carry stocks of sample rolls they will open to show you a large spread of pattern. This way you can see how it will look on your wall at home.

Before you start

If you're planning a complete redecoration which includes painting the woodwork and ceiling, it's best to complete those jobs before you commence papering.

Now that you're ready, check you have all the tools. There's a list on page 24. Next, unwrap a roll of wallpaper and read the instructions.

Measure and cut your first 'drop' or strip, allowing 100 mm extra paper at the ceiling and floor.

If you're using prepasted paper be sure your trough is filled with lukewarm water and placed adjacent to the wall. For unpasted paper you will need a sturdy table or bench on which to work and mix the paste.

Next step is to use a plumb line so you will have a vertical line from ceiling to floor. Never use the corner of a room, door or window as your guide; they are seldom absolutely square.

Take the plumb line and suspend the weight from a high point on the wall, about 480 mm from a door or corner. Wait until it is stationary and, with your pencil, mark clearly under the line in three places. Draw a line to join the marks using your straightedge as a guide.

Now you have a starting place and you're ready to hang your wallpaper.

 GREEN TIP
When preparing surfaces for papering, wear suitable protective clothing. Protect your eyes when sanding and wear a mask to prevent inhaling harmful substances.

Wall preparation

Preparing walls for wallpapering is not difficult. However, like any successful project you tackle around the home, it is an important step and well worth the effort.

Laura Ashley

You should aim for clean, non-porous surfaces. Porous surfaces should be avoided because they 'steal' moisture from the paste, affecting its adhesive qualities.

If possible, remove blinds and curtains, wall lights and, of course, prints and pictures! Give yourself as much room as possible in which to work by moving furniture to another room or placing it in the centre. Use drop sheets to protect your floor coverings – old bed sheets are ideal.

Painted surfaces

Test for porosity by wetting a small area with a sponge and seeing if there's rapid evaporation; you can tell by watching the edge of the area you've moistened. If it contracts quickly the chances are you have a porous surface. To remedy, simply apply a coat of size.

Glossy painted surfaces should be rubbed down with a coarse-grade sandpaper to provide a key, then sized.

Flaking and powdery painted walls must be well rubbed down and washed using sugar soap. If the powdery condition persists, apply a sealer, allow to dry then size. Ensure good ventilation.

Unpainted plasterboard or Gyprock

Prime with a coat of oil sealer. This makes it possible to remove the wallpaper at a later date without destroying the surface of the plasterboard or Gyprock. The sealer also eliminates porosity. Allow to dry thoroughly.

New plaster walls

If your walls are newly plastered be sure they are

Above: Country kitchen with striped wallpaper

Removing dry-peelable wallpaper – inserting craft knife under corner (right); pulling paper off wall (below right)

Using a steam stripper to strip wallpaper

completely dry before applying wallpaper. New plaster walls may also have 'hot spots' caused by lime in the plaster mix. These can be neutralised by applying a solution of 1 kg of zinc sulphate in 4.5 litres of water. Sandpaper lightly then apply a coat of sealer. Allow to dry before finishing with a coat of size.

Painted plaster walls

Remove loose paint using coarse-grade sandpaper (an electric sander is ideal but wear protective goggles and mask). Cover cracks and nail holes with filler and sand smooth. If existing paint is gloss, sand the surface until it dulls. Apply size to all walls prior to papering.

Cement render

Lining paper must be used on all cement render surfaces. Before hanging, fill any cracks and holes and rub the walls down with a Carborundum block to remove any nibs and loose particles. The walls should then be coated

with an oil-based masonry sealer and allowed to dry before lining.

Wallpapered walls

Remove old wallcoverings before applying new wallpaper. Dry strippable, fabric-backed and vinyl wallcoverings are easily removed by loosening corners and pulling the strips gently off the walls.

There are a couple of methods by which non-strippable wallpapers can be removed:
❏ Scoring the surface with coarse-grade sandpaper then applying one of the wallcovering solutions available from wallpaper retailers for the purpose. Apply the solution with a sponge, allow it to soak, then remove the paper with a scraper.
❏ A steamer which can be hired from most wallpaper stores. This is very effective and requires less effort! Washable or painted paper must be scored first to allow the steam to penetrate.

Treating mildew

Mildew is a fungus growth usually found in damp areas such as bathrooms, kitchens, basements and wardrobes. Its cause is a combination of three conditions: darkness, moisture and organic material on which to feed. It can appear on walls as yellow, green, orange, grey or black spots.

Many adhesives and wall sizes today have mildew inhibitors in their formulae. Household bleach used undiluted will remove mildew. There are fungicides available too which will remove the problem. However, their use requires care and caution.

Always wear protective rubber gloves and ensure the room is well ventilated. You must treat the initial cause of mildew and mould otherwise they will recur.

Stripping old wallpaper – wetting wallpaper with a sponge

Above and below: Using a stripping knife to strip paper

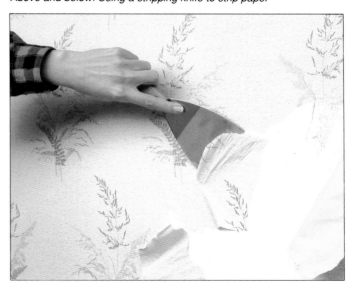

Skill class
Hanging prepasted wallpaper

Which room first?

It's not unusual, if you are wall-papering for the first time, to choose a small room in which to start ... just in case! In most cases that means a bathroom or toilet. The advice from the experts is ... don't ! You'll have a cistern, shower recess, bath, wash basin, cabinet and all sorts of other odd-shaped fittings to contend with.

It's much easier to begin in a bedroom or lounge where the walls are uninterrupted, allowing you to quickly polish your skills. By the time you reach the bathroom, you'll be an expert!

Prior to hanging your first strip, check which pattern match is appropriate. Do this by placing two rolls on a table, or the floor, and noting where the design matches.

On a straight-across-match the pattern will be the same distance from the ceiling on every strip. Drop-match designs alternate with every other strip. For the latter style, cut strips from alternate rolls to save wastage.

To begin papering, cut a strip of wallpaper that will reach from ceiling to floor, or skirting board, allowing an extra 100 mm top and bottom for trimming.

Roll the strip with the pattern side in, taking care that you roll from the bottom so that the top (the end that will go nearest the ceiling) is on the outside. Place the rolled strip in the water trough (containing lukewarm water) for at least 15 seconds to enable the water to activate the film of paste on the back of the paper.

Feed the top of the strip under the guide on the trough and pull it up slowly to ensure both sides are evenly soaked.

If you need a stepladder, make sure it's already in position. Hang the first strip with the vertical edge against the plumb line you have already marked on the wall. Place the paper against the wall near the ceiling then smooth it down with a clean wet sponge or plastic smoothing plane (see steps 3 and 4 on page 31).

Use a firm action. Start in the centre of the strip and move outwards to the edges to re-move the large bubbles; the small ones will disappear as the wallpaper dries. Remove sur-plus paste from the surface before it dries. Don't forget to sponge away paste from the ceiling and skirting board too.

If you find you're taking some time to get a strip in place, don't panic! Prepasted wallpaper is quite forgiving and you'll find there's ample time to manoeuvre it.

As you slide the strip into position, avoid placing your hands too close to the edges. This prevents overstretching the wallpaper, which may otherwise pull back as it dries, leaving an open seam.

With the knife, trim the excess paper from the bottom and top using the straightedge as a guide; then smooth the ends down with your sponge.

It's a good idea to continue trimming as you go and to change the water and rinse the sponge frequently so you avoid a build-up of paste.

Hang the next strip in the same way. This time, however, you'll be matching the design and creating a seam. With your fingertips, slide the wallpaper gently up or down until the pattern is aligned and the strip butts up against the edge of the first piece. Don't overlap it.

Continue wallpapering in this way.

Papering corners

Internal corners of most rooms are rarely true and so the wallpaper should be hung in two strips. Cut the last strip going into the corner so that 15 mm will wrap around to the next wall. Make a new plumb line on the unpapered wall and hang the next strip so it overlaps the 15 mm strip from the previous piece.

External corners should be approached in much the same

BUTT SEAM

What sort of seam?

The best way of joining seams when you're hang-ing wallpaper is the 'butt' method. To butt a seam, hang your wallpaper so the edges of the strips fit tightly together with no overlap. The finished result is a flat, invisible seam, with no double thickness.

Laura Ashley

Blue and white wallpaper in a country-style setting offset by a natural timber sideboard

way but allow a 50 mm wrap-around. If some curling occurs on the overlap, use a latex adhesive to stick it down.

1 Use a plumb line to get the verticals

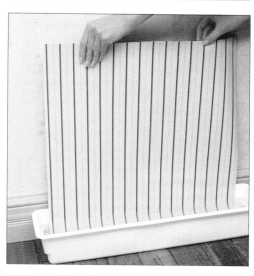

2 Take the first strip out of the water trough

3 Use a smoothing plane to smooth out wrinkles

4 Smooth wallpaper along skirting board

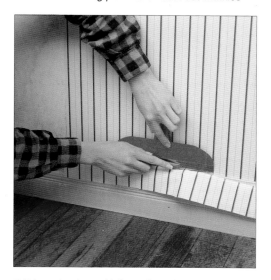

5 Trim strip along skirting using a broad knife

6 Use a sponge to remove excess paste

Electricity outlets

Before you work around any electrical socket, switch or similar fitting, turn off the power supply at the mains.

Hang the paper over the switch or socket and smooth the length as neatly as possible. Make diagonal cuts across the centre of the switch to each corner so the cuts form four triangles. Peel back the flaps and trim off, then smooth the edges against the switch.

Light fittings and centrepieces

Many older homes have attractive decorative plaster centrepieces. Paper in the normal manner and, as you reach the decoration, cut a series of long flaps in the strip which will allow you to tuck the paper in around the edge.

Most rooms have pendant (overhead) lights. Before hanging, measure and mark on the back of the strip the position of the fitting.

From the centre of this point make a series of cuts in a star shape. When you reach the light, pass the fitting through the hole and continue to the end of the strip. Return to the light and smooth the paper around the fitting where it's attached to the ceiling, trimming off the excess.

Use a similar system of 'star' cuts to fit wallpaper round circular light switches and other fittings.

**Warning!
Before cutting around light switches and outlets, turn off the electricity and don't turn the power back on until the paste is dry.**

Wallpapering around light fittings

1 Cut the diagonals around the light switch

2 Trim the paper

Doors and windows

Hang the length next to a door frame, sponging down the butt joint so the pattern lines up. Leave the other edge to loosely over-lap the door. In the excess, make a diagonal cut towards the top corner of the frame and use your straightedge to crease the waste against the door frame. Smooth down and trim excess.

Treat windows the same as doors. If the window is set into a reveal, hang the strip next to the window, allowing it to overhang. Make a horizontal cut just above the edge of the window reveal and another near the bottom. Fold the paper around to cover the reveal; crease with the straightedge and trim.

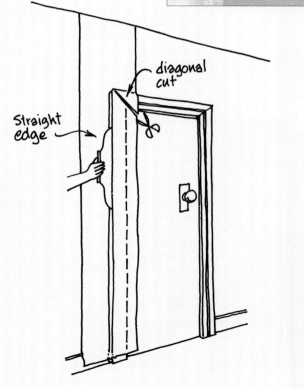

Though much of the wallpaper sold today is prepasted, there is still some which will need paste applied before hanging.

To do the job you need a fairly narrow table or trestle, a soft wall brush or pasting brush and a plastic bucket.

Follow the mixing instructions for the paste. Make sure it's not lumpy by adding a small amount at a time to the water, and allow it to stand before using.

Cut your strip of wallpaper and lay on the table with the pattern face down.

Dip the brush in the paste and apply to the wallpaper, brushing out from the centre. Be sure to cover the edges.

Slightly overlap the edge of the table with the paper so that paste is not transferred from it to the front surface.

Now fold the pasted piece back on itself. Move the surplus paper onto the table and do the other half in the same way.

Fold the strip in on itself again, making sure the last fold is the top of the piece.

Leave the pasted strip as long as necessary for it to soak up the paste and for the wallpaper to become supple. If you don't there is a risk of bubbles occurring. While you wait, do several more strips.

Carry your folded strip to the wall, unfold the top piece and hang as you would prepasted wallpaper.

Hanging wallpaper on the ceiling can give your room a totally new look – it can either be a continuation of a pattern on the walls, or the only surface in the room that's papered.

Overlap to wall covered later when wall is papered

Work backwards with other person supporting folded paper

Chalk line parallel to main window wall and one "paper width" in from wall

Skill Class
Papering a ceiling

You can achieve some spectacular results by papering a ceiling and it certainly adds a 'total' look to any room. Nurseries and older children's rooms can be lots of fun for the occupants. One make of wallpaper available for ceilings has tiny stars which glow in the dark (see page 35)!

To calculate how much paper is needed use the table on page 27 as an approximate guide.

The basic technique for papering a ceiling is much the same as for walls; however, it is much easier if you have someone to assist.

You also need to comfortably reach the ceiling so a sturdy platform is essential. A plank spanning two stepladders and strong enough to support two people is ideal. A single stepladder is not recommended.

Because the strips of wallpaper for a ceiling are usually much longer than for walls a table top or similar level surface on which to work is helpful.

Just like walls the ceiling needs to be clean and the surface sound. If in doubt, apply a coat of size after cleaning. The experts recommend starting parallel with the main window of the room and working away from the light so seams are not obvious.

Mark a guide line on the ceiling for the position of the first strip. It will be one roll's width out from the wall.

Cut the strip the full length of the ceiling allowing 100 mm for trimming and 5 mm for an overlap onto the wall. When you eventually paper the wall this will be covered. The overlap is also handy to conceal any cracks where walls join the ceiling.

Roll the paper in the usual way and place it in the water trough. Remove slowly and draw the roll onto the table folding it in a concertina fashion with folds about half a metre wide.

You and your assistant will both need to mount the trestle and you'll actually be working backwards! Place the first fold against the ceiling; as you smooth the paper your helper works behind you, unfolding as you progress.

Borders

Friezes, or borders as they are better known, are among the oldest forms of decorating. They can be found on the walls inside the great pyramids in Egypt and amid the ruins of ancient Pompeii.

Today they are just as popular and have led a revival of interest in all wallcoverings. To begin with, borders are inexpensive and simple to apply and remove. And they're low risk, especially for do-it-yourself decorators who may be a little cautious. Success with a border, however, frequently leads to a feeling of confidence and the next step is to paper an entire room.

The sheer variety of borders available these days is breathtaking. Their popularity is such that manufacturers are producing pattern books devoted entirely to borders. Borders are also a big part of coordinate ranges which feature wallpaper, matching fabrics and companion borders. The overall effect is remarkable.

The tools you'll need are the same as for wallpapering and the same rules apply for wall preparation. Aim for a clean surface.

Measuring is easy too. It's all done in linear metres, so you simply measure the distance around a room – if you are going around a door then measure the sides and top too. Most borders are sold in 5 or 10 m lengths so you get plenty for your money! They are usually prepasted and so you use the water trough as you would with full-sized wallpaper.

Cut the desired length, roll and place in the water for no more than 15 seconds. Slowly remove and fold with pasted side to pasted side for about three minutes. Reroll the border with the pattern on the outside and position one end on the wall.

Carefully unroll with one hand while you smooth and remove bubbles with the other. Allow an overlap in a corner or around a door. As you complete a strip, stand back and check the border is where you want it to be. If you're happy with it, sponge away any surplus paste and move onto the next strip.

Applying borders around doors and windows allows you to either overlap where they join, or to mitre the corners. To mitre, overlap the ends of two intersecting border strips and make a 45° diagonal cut using your knife and straightedge. Peel away the excess and smooth the

Colour-coordinated butterfly border, wallpaper and curtains

join with your sponge or smoothing plane. Fold unpasted borders concertina-fashion after pasting.

Borders can work wonders for virtually any room. Use them to accentuate a picture rail by placing the border above or below the rail. And if the room doesn't have one then create the illusion by applying your border at picture rail height! You can highlight a cornice or make your own.

Perhaps the most dramatic effect borders achieve is when they are used at chair rail height. The range of decorating options open to you is unlimited using this decorating device.

You can wallpaper below or above the border and paint the other half (do your painting first), or use two different but complementary wallpapers and have the

Sweet-pea wallpaper in a bedroom

border intersecting them.

There's nothing to stop you applying a border over the top of wallpaper to provide focal points. If you have a prized mirror, painting or print, use a border to give it added importance in your home. You can even apply them to ceilings for a very distinctive designer look!

Children's rooms and nurseries should be bright, cheerful places. The variety of borders available for kids is endless and ranges from alphabets to fantasy characters and cartoon favourites.

Who said borders have to be only on walls and ceilings? Use them to decorate screens, doors, cupboards, toy and craft boxes, kitchen canisters and other containers. The choice is yours.

Novelties

It seems that ever since our prehistoric ancestors decorated their caves with ochre paintings of the wild creatures they hunted, we've been fascinated with decorating the walls of our homes. We're no

different today except the options are a little wider!

As well as the myriad ranges of wallpapers and borders, there are dozens of novelty items from wall-sized murals to tiny stickers. For children, especially, the choice is huge. They can personalise their bedroom and play areas using animal stickers or cartoon characters. Parents can even keep a tab on junior's growth with a height chart in the shape of a giraffe! And of course there are those borders and wallpapers that glow when the lights go off!

The first murals were mediaeval tapestries, which depicted great moments in history such as battles and conquests. These days you can transform a dull den or unadorned family room into the great outdoors with giant floor-to-ceiling murals showing alpine meadows, Nordic forests or a palm-fringed tropical beach!

'Glo to sleep' wallpaper and border – daytime

'Glo to sleep' wallpaper and border – night-time

Below: Child's nursery

35

25 Great decorating tips

1 To ensure a coordinated look in a room, approximate the colour of your furnishings and floor coverings then use the colour wheel or a colour card to help you choose the right wall and accent colours. Some major paint manufacturers have colour cards which show colours arranged in pairs – when used together, the colours within a pair will form a harmonious combination. You may also select a colour from one pair and combine it with colours from surrounding pairs.

2 Window walls will appear darker as they only receive reflected light. Ceilings always look darker than walls painted the same colour.

3 If you have problem walls with an imperfect surface full of cracks, why not use a paint-over wallcovering? This type of wallcovering has a textured pattern which you then paint over with two coats of a water-based acrylic paint of your choice. Simply prepare walls as per normal - all surfaces should be smooth and cracks and irregularities filled; then follow the manufacturer's instructions.

4 Don't underestimate the power of a new colour scheme to revive timber cupboards and shelves! Give everything a good clean with sugar soap to begin with, including cupboard interiors. Undercoat cupboards and shelves then finish with two topcoats of a hardwearing gloss paint – white is hard to beat for cupboard interiors as it lightens and brightens. Paint the cupboard doors too – choose a colour you are happy with, perhaps one that features in the kitchen

already, or one that you intend to redecorate with.

5 Try a spattered or stippled black wall as the perfect backdrop to a collection of framed black-and-white photographs.

6 Strong colours cleverly put together spell confidence – but it is important to balance the tones for the right mix. Try emerald and sapphire side by side with accents of gold on accessories. Look for prints that incorporate the scheme's colours.

7 Hot spicy colours combine to give a rich, warm look. Choose a vermilion rose colour and cooler shades for accents with terracotta, pale wood and brass accessories.

8 Neutrals are so easy on the eye – try beige on

beige, or grey on grey, or go one step further and mix them together! Use a fabric that incorporates both colours and choose a warm soft apricot shade as your accent colour.

9 Black is beautiful – try black with bright primaries like red and yellow to bring it to life. Choose a satin finish paint to reflect light.

10 The great colour swatch – take a tip and always look at your swatches in the room they're intended for; don't try to 'remember' a colour – always carry a swatch; look at swatches on the plane

they are to be used on, e.g. lay carpet samples on the floor, hold curtain fabric to the light, etc.

11 If one of your furnishing fabrics contains many colours, pick your scheme from these – you already know they work well together. But too many colours in a scheme can look too bitty – only choose two or three plus an accent colour.

12 Strong patterns mix, providing the colours are carefully coordinated. When mixing patterns, make

36

sure the main colours are used in equal proportions for other areas, such as the walls and floor.

13 Soothing pastel colours help to create an airy feeling in the bathroom and have a 'clean' look about them. Choose colours of equal depth of tone – don't let one colour dominate. Try a strong blue as an accent colour.

14 Colour can be used to play visual tricks on the eye – use pale colours in small rooms to reflect the light, giving an impression of more space; use darker shades or warmer colours to bring the walls in for a cosier feel; to 'lower' a high ceiling

which is dwarfing the furniture, paint the ceiling a slightly darker colour than the walls – if you have a picture rail, continue painting down the walls as far as the rail; to broaden a narrow hallway with a high ceiling, aim for a darker colour on ceiling and floor, and a lighter one on the walls.

15 Make a swatch board to test out your colour ideas. Find samples of fabric or paint similar to the existing colours and designs, i.e. things you won't be changing, like a sofa or a carpet. Cut the samples to the same proportions they'll be in the finished scheme, e.g. a large paint swatch for walls and a small one for woodwork.

Find a large sheet of white

card and use as the swatch board (it's important to mount the samples on white as a coloured ground won't give a true picture). Clip the samples to the board then sort through all your new samples and place each onto the swatch board to see its effects.

Test accent colour ideas by using strands of wool or cotton in various colours. On-the-spot reference is crucial so don't forget to carry the swatch board around with you on shopping trips.

16 Use gingham and floral-stripe wallpaper for country cottage looks.

17 Separate patterns with a white-painted dado.

18 Counterpoint heavy woodwork with Wedgwood blue and cream.

19 To emphasise a textured wall, graze the surface with light using downlighters installed about

200 mm away from the wall. Use fixtures with a non-reflective internal surface, and 60 to 150 watt bulbs.

20 Yellow will create a happy, welcoming feeling and has the effect of coming forward from the walls; it works particularly well in cold, dark rooms. Soft, butter tones mix beautifully with antique furniture, especially of the Regency period.

21 Add a dado rail to break up a plain cube of a room. Paint the rail and other woodwork with a rich strong colour.

22 Try some variations on a theme for wallpaper treatments – comics for kids' rooms; old telephone directories and magazine articles for a study; magazine recipe pages for a kitchen. Use coloured paints and polyurethane or clear varnish to create an arty decoupage effect by building up layers of images.

23 Very subtle printed-texture and paint-effect patterns are easy to decorate with as they can be mixed with more definite patterns, show marks less easily than plain fabrics and feature a range of colours to suit most schemes. A masonry sealer applied to porous bricks will help to prevent excessive absorption.

24 Thinking of painting over brickwork? Not all bricks are suitable for this treatment – bricks should be sound and well-burnt, with low water-absorption qualities.

25 Composite design – try a mixture of colour, pattern and texture outside your home as well as inside, with a two-colour paint scheme on timber and brickwork and the added interest and contrast of latticework and trellising.

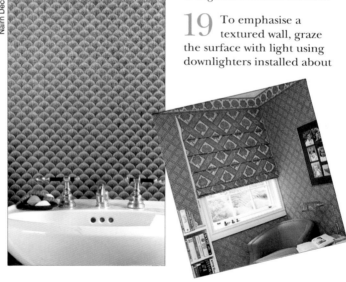

Nairn Decor

Dulux

If you are intending to revamp your house using decorative paint finishes, you are embarking on the most exciting and rewarding of all refurbishment. You will achieve the most stylish results using processes which can be as cheap as the cost of the paint!

DECORATIVE PAINT FINISHES

You are now entering a world where nothing is really what it seems – fantasy abounds – and you'll find that it is possible, after all, to turn that sow's ear into a silk purse!

The rough, cold cement floor now looks and feels like expensive inlaid stone blocks, costing nothing but your physical labour and a few tins of paint. Walls of a boring dark hall have metamorphosed into a gem-like Wedgwood box with the application of paint and some cheap plastic ornaments.

A room – apparently panelled silk – is, in fact, just a cheap paint finish once more. Pale, subtle colour glows in soft dragged lines on surfaces which previously were flat and dead and of no interest. With your labour, some paint and a lot of enthusiasm, you can turn your house into a treasure house of colour, texture and warmth, envied by all.

Special paint effects used to be the province of skilled professional decorators – but not anymore! You can texture and colour your walls, woodwork and furniture in ways that will make them unique – and you can do it simply and on-the-cheap!

You can achieve broken colour finishes by using two very basic methods: a paint glaze is either added over a background colour – with a sponge, or by spattering, for example; or the paint glaze is rolled or painted onto the background colour and then partially removed using rags, combs, stippling brushes and so on. Different tools produce quite different effects – and the way you manipulate each tool is all-important.

The colour and pattern you choose can add that really magical – and often missing – element of style to a room's colour scheme. They create wonderful illusions – the overall effect can look luxurious and very expensive, yet the process can be as cheap as the cost of the paint!

These finishes are suited to articles made from just about anything – including wood, glass, ceramics, highly glazed pottery, leather *and* plastic. Plastic items bought straight off the shelf from a supermarket or department store – a plastic jug, tray or wastepaper basket – can be very successfully transformed and stylised with a painted finish.

So many of the everyday objects that surround us can be completely re-created using painted finishes – old table mats, vases and tin canisters to name a few. Don't forget that these things all fit into your larger design and colour scheme and can, in fact, add that essential 'just right' finishing touch.

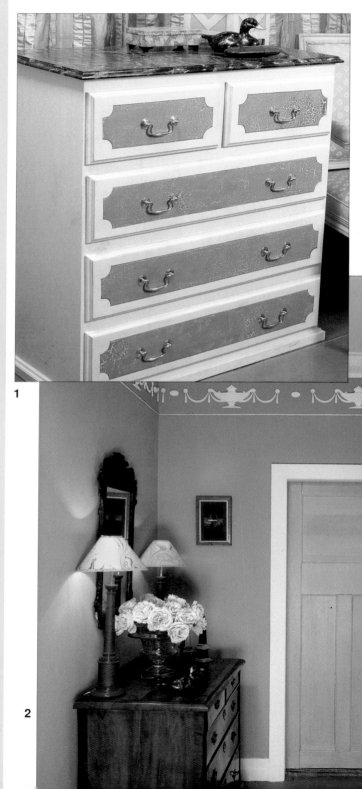

1

2

GREEN TIP
NEW LOOKS FOR OLD

It is much more environmentally sound to give an old piece of furniture a new lease of life, or to restore a section of your house using recycled timber. It's too easy to fall into the 'disposable' habit. Always look at second-hand alternatives – you may save precious resources as well as valuable cash.

Things are often discarded when all they need is a coat of paint and a special finish. If you do decide to discard an old piece of furniture, offer it to a charity, or have a garage (car boot) sale.

1 Whitewood chest of drawers with a faux marbre top and crackle medium finish (see p.43)

2 Wedgwood green hallway with trompe l'oeil door (see p.41)

3 Blue room with ragged and dragged walls and a stone-finished floor (see p.42 and p.47)

4 Detail of stone-finished floor (p.42)

5 Stippling (see p.44)

6 Parchment finish (see p.45)

7 Sponging (see p.45)

8 Simple marbling (see p.47)

9 Dragging (see p.44)

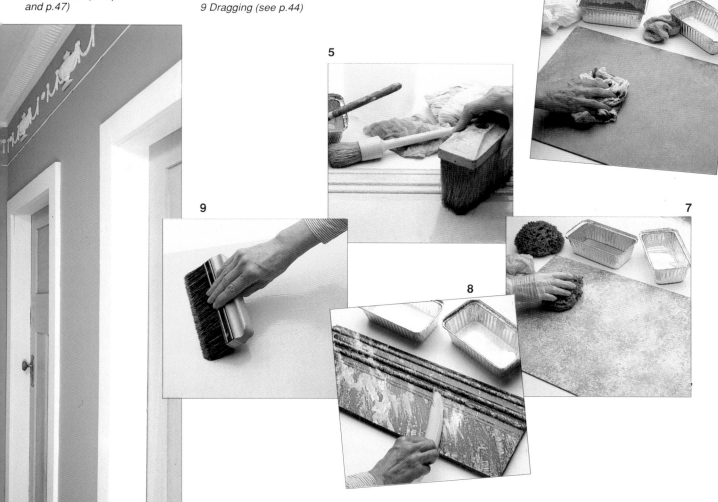

Tools and supplies

To achieve the best results, good tools and supplies are of prime importance. Buy them as you need them – start with the basics and keep on adding as your skills improve and you take on more ambitious projects.

- ❑ eggshell enamel (one part matt (flat) enamel to one part satin enamel or one part matt (flat) acrylic to one part satin acrylic)
- ❑ matt (flat) enamel paints
- ❑ water-based artists' acrylics
- ❑ universal tints
- ❑ oil-based and water-based scumble medium
- ❑ turps (white spirit)
- ❑ shellac
- ❑ rollers
- ❑ methylated spirits
- ❑ roller covers
- ❑ roller pans (trays)
- ❑ wall stipple brush (rectangular)
- ❑ cutting-in (detail) brush, 50 mm
- ❑ 50 mm to 75 mm paint brushes
- ❑ dragging brush
- ❑ round stipple brush
- ❑ natural sponges
- ❑ calico (cut and washed) – buy new calico, cut in 20 m lengths, then wash, put through dryer to remove lint, and cut into short lengths
- ❑ containers for mixing
- ❑ large stirring sticks
- ❑ strainer bags (nylon tights)
- ❑ duster brush
- ❑ tack rags
- ❑ ladders
- ❑ lint-free dust cloths
- ❑ masking tape and tape dispenser
- ❑ razor blades

Cleaning tools

Most painting tools can be cleaned first by soaking in turps (white spirit) if oil-based, then by washing in hot, soapy water. If using water-based paints, hot soapy water followed by rinsing will do the trick. Rinse thoroughly – tools will harden and become useless if any paint residue is left after washing.

❑ All brushes must be carefully rinsed after use. Have two or three tins of turps (white spirit) ready (see our Green Tip for recycling).

❑ To soften a hardened brush, dip it into a saucepan of boiling water, detergent and ammonia – or immerse in paint stripper or brush cleaner for a short time.

The work area

The ideal work area is light, airy and spacious – with lots of shelving, cupboards and storage space. If this sounds too idyllic for your circumstances, don't despair – you can also get by with a very basic set-up.

❑ If you are short on space, an efficient work area can be created by fitting out a cupboard with shelves and using a card table which can be folded away when necessary.

❑ Remember too that many of the painting and varnishing materials that you will be using are highly flammable – so if you set up work in your kitchen, stay well away from the cooking area.

❑ Ventilation is very important – you need a constant flow of fresh air to disperse any potentially dangerous fumes.

❑ Keep your work area as clean as possible – stray dust and grime can ruin a freshly painted surface.

❑ Good lighting is essential. Fit an extra light overhead if you don't have good natural light.

❑ A set of shelves close at hand is an extra bonus for storage of tools and supplies which you need to lay your hands on quickly and easily.

GREEN TIP

To recycle turps (white spirit), take a plastic or metal kitchen strainer, remove the handle (this is easier to do with a plastic strainer), make three or four S-shaped hangers from a wire coathanger and suspend the strainer on these in a large tin of turps (white spirit). When you wash brushes, the sludge from the paint will sink to the bottom of the tin and the turps (white spirit) remains clean.

You will find this system enables you to use the same turps (white spirit) for months. When you have been using this system for a while you can empty the turps (white spirit) into another container, clean out the sludge from the bottom and then replace the old turps (white spirit). This also means that it is possible to leave a brush standing in the turps (white spirit) overnight, supported by the strainer. Don't leave the brush sitting in the sludge at the bottom of the tin!

A selection of brushes

Preparation

The essence of the perfect painted finish lies in its preparation.

All walls should be sanded back and, where necessary, filled. A wonderful filler for large holes in walls is cornice glue. This is in powder form and may be bought in bulk and made up following the instructions on the packet. It is an excellent filler and sands beautifully, so that the patching is not evident. If this is not obtainable, any good wall filler will do the job.

Once the filler is dry and sanded so that the filling is imperceptible, the filled area must be sealed. If you do not seal the filled area, you will find it shows through as a grey patch when you later apply the antiquing glaze.

Shellac is a sealing medium. It is thinned with methylated spirits and dries almost immediately, so that one can get on with the painting job straightaway. If shellac is not available, use whatever sealer you can buy at your local supplier's. It is most important that the walls are well sanded and made as smooth as possible.

Once the wall is in as good a condition as you can possibly achieve and all sanding has been completed, wipe down with cotton rags and vacuum the floor and walls. Then wipe all over with tack rags. These are made of cheesecloth impregnated with linseed oil and are invaluable for removing final dust.

Before painting the walls, make sure that all areas which are not to be painted are masked – this will save hours of cleaning up later. Only buy good quality masking tape – never buy masking tape which does not bear a brand name or which is on sale because it is old stock.

Wall glazing

If you are restoring old walls, or new for that matter, great care must be given to the preparation. As with so many aspects of interior and exterior decoration, the better the preparation, the better the final product.

Essential tools
❏ roller trays
❏ low tack tape
❏ also see tools and supplies listed opposite

You may now start painting the walls with eggshell sheen enamel. The colour is your decision, but generally a room or a whole house can happily be prepared in white eggshell sheen enamel and then any colour or colours imposed over the white. If you cannot buy this style of paint, you can easily make it yourself by mixing one part matt (flat) enamel with one part satin enamel, thus creating the slight sheen one sees on an eggshell (see page 43 for making up your own).

If you do not wish to work in oil-based paints, you may create the same eggshell in acrylic house paints. However, a word of warning: when applying a decorative paint glaze to walls, the glaze is more workable and stays 'open' (does not dry out immediately) longer if it is imposed on an oil-based paint rather than on an acrylic paint. Acrylic paints are very absorbent and tend to soak up a decorative paint glaze in a very thirsty manner and make it much more difficult to work.

When applying the paint to the walls you may use a brush or a roller. Rollers are

very quick, but tend to leave behind the appearance of an orange skin. To overcome this 'orange-peel' appearance, lay on one section with the roller about 610 mm at a time then quickly come back over the wet paint with a good bristle brush and 'lay-off', that is, pull the brush from the ceiling down to the skirting board through the paint, laying off and removing the orange peel pattern in the paint. If you do this carefully the paint surface should be absolutely smooth.

Doors, architraves, skirting boards, windows, etc, should be prepared in the same way, using a brush to apply the paint. After the

BEFORE

AFTER

WEDGWOOD GREEN HALLWAY
This once drab hallway has been transformed into an elegant entrance with creative paint finishes.

Plastic copies of 18th century carved wooden mouldings have been glued to the walls and painted white against solid Wedgwood green walls. The trompe l'oeil door has been dragged and finished in a stone colour then shading has been cleverly added to give the appearance of panelling.

Note: Enamel is an oil-based paint and can be matt (flat), satin or high gloss.

Warning!
Many paint materials are highly flammable and should be used away from any heat source.

TIPSTRIP

MASKING TAPE
One of the most deadly paint removers is masking tape.
❏ Always remember that masking tape left on windows which are subject to sunlight will become immovable in a very short time, finally requiring scraping, or acetone, to remove.
❏ Try to get the painting job completed as quickly as possible. Leave until touch dry – no longer – then carefully remove the masking tape. Don't rip – very carefully and slowly pull off at a 45° angle.

application of two coats of eggshell enamel the walls may look opaque. If this is the case, you are then ready to get on with the decorative paint glaze. If, however, there are patches on the wall which have a slightly grey appearance, you must apply more coats of eggshell until the wall is absolutely opaque.

Once the walls are solid colour they are ready for you to apply the decorative paint glaze. Another word of warning here. If, despite all your hard work, it has not been possible to get an absolutely even, smooth surface on your walls, there are some paint glazes which will not be suitable for it.

The one finish in this series which would be unsuitable for a wall with surface irregularities is a dragged finish. This finish requires a very smooth, even surface, so that the brush may glide over the wall and not meet any bumps, which would cause the finish to appear uneven and look as though the painter acquired a bad case of the wobbles.

The walls are now ready to receive the decorative paint glaze. You must first remask. Masking skirting boards, cornices, architraves and doors is absolutely essential if you are to achieve first-class, professional finishes. Any area which is not to receive the paint glaze *must* be masked off. Use a low tack tape which is one half low tack and the other half plain brown paper. This tape is made for French polishers and is less likely to pull off the finish than more traditional tapes. The fact that one half of the tape is plain paper is very useful as it will provide extra protection to masked areas. Be careful, however, at corners where it does not bond well to itself, and use

traditional tape over it to make sure the bonding is secure at that point.

You will find that if you take the trouble and time to do all this masking, the decorative paint finish will be crisp and clean on all the edges and you will have no cleaning up to do. Ignore this step and you will spend hours removing unwanted paint glaze from other areas.

Before commencing work on the walls, spend some time working on sample boards so that you get the feel of creating a paint finish. If you have a wall or two on which to practise, such as a lavatory or laundry area (they can always be repainted!), try the finishes on those walls first before moving on to a more ambitious project.

Woodwork

In Victorian and Edwardian houses, the colour in woodwork was often made by aniline dyes suspended in either shellac or varnish. This dye will bleed through almost any paint finish.

To determine if the

Sanding

Sealing

colour is, in fact, aniline, take some steel wool and methylated spirits and rub the finish vigorously. If the finish starts to come away and some colour appears to be remaining in the wood, you can be sure it is aniline. Similarly, if the finish is varnish with aniline, steel wool soaked in turps (white spirit) used in the same way will give you the same answer.

The only material which will contain these dyes is an aluminium paint. This paint is readily available for painting roofs and is invaluable for covering aniline. Follow the directions on the tin for application. Make sure the background is completely covered with the aluminium paint before proceeding to the next step of applying eggshell.

Furniture

If the piece of furniture has been well painted, varnished or French-polished, there is no need to strip it. If, however, it is a mess of dripping paint, remove the offending cover first.

STONE-FINISHED FLOOR

This once raw concrete floor has been painted to suit the room's soft colours and delicate textures. The concrete was first sealed with shellac, then three colours were ragged and sponged on to create the texture and appearance of stone. The floor has then been finished with 'lining' to make a stone-tiled pattern.

AFTER

BEFORE

If the first case applies, sand back the piece until it is smooth. Fill any areas which require filling, then seal filled areas with shellac or a proprietary sealer. Sand the sealed area until it is smooth, wipe with a cotton rag and then a tack cloth and begin painting with either oil or acrylic eggshell sheen, usually white.

If the piece of furniture has been stripped, then it must be treated as raw and first sealed with shellac or a proprietary sealer. Sand as above and wipe off – then coat with the usual coats of eggshell sheen to an opaque coverage.

You are then ready to apply the decorative paint glaze.

Glazes

In painted finishes, glaze does not mean shiny. A glaze is a semi-translucent coat of paint painted onto an opaque background. The paint is broken open with a tool, allowing the opaque background to shine through, thus creating depth and dimension. Consequently,

these finishes are often referred to as 'broken' paint finishes. If you wish to create a shine on the finish, this is done by applying varnish – either satin or gloss.

Oil-based glaze
❏ one part matt (flat) enamel
❏ one part scumble medium (see below)
❏ one or two parts turps (white spirit)

Water-based glaze
❏ one part matt (flat) acrylic paint
❏ one part water-based scumble medium
❏ water, depending upon finish to be executed

Scumble medium or antiquing glaze
Scumble medium is a semi-translucent medium composed of linseed oil, turps (white spirit), whiting and extenders to create a longer drying time.

Scumble medium is an essential part of glazing. It adds translucency to the paint, extends the drying time – which means you have more time to work with the paint once it has been applied – and enables the paint to hold the imprint of the tool. If you did not use

scumble medium and performed, say, a stipple, you would find the paint had closed up into an opaque colour within an hour or two.

Oil-based and water-based scumble medium both have the same properties, although water-based is obviously made from entirely different materials.

Overglaze
This is a wonderful means of softening or brightening a finish.

❏ one part oil-based paint (usually white with a drop of the background colour)
❏ one part oil-based scumble medium
❏ eight parts turps (white spirit)

The finish on which you wish to apply the overglaze should have dried overnight. Apply the overglaze with a brush or a roller, stippling to remove any brush or roller strokes, and then start texturing with a piece of washed lint-free cotton.

Allow some of the background to shine through. Do not cover the background completely with the overglaze – the application is simply to

Mixing eggshell sheen

Applying eggshell sheen

soften or enliven. Make sure you pick up any drips with the cotton.

The overglaze will be absorbed into the background quite easily and you will find it adds a lovely amorphous quality to the original glaze.

BEFORE

WHITEWOOD CHEST OF DRAWERS
This pine chest of drawers has been sealed with shellac and painted cream. Panels have been painted on the drawers and finished with crackle medium. The top has a faux marbre finish which adds the classical finishing touch to the whole piece. (See Skill Class on page 46 for crackle-finished panels.)

AFTER

Skill Class
Stippling

If using water-based mediums, add one part glaze to two parts water. You must always use your common sense when thinning, as the viscosity of paint and scumble medium can vary dramatically. The glaze should always sit on the background as a cover and not as texture. If you find there is texture in the glaze, it is too thick and you will need to thin it.

Oil-based glaze
❑ one part matt (flat) enamel
❑ one part scumble medium
❑ one to two parts turps
 (white spirit)

Tools
❑ roller or brush to apply the glaze
❑ rectangular wall stipple brush

Quickly apply the glaze to the background, leaving a ragged edge where stopping the

1 Apply the glaze to skirting board

2 Bounce the brush up and down into the glaze to create a stippled effect

application (this is in case the edge dries out and you get a seam line – a ragged seam line is less obvious than a straight join). Now bounce the brush up and down into the glaze, imposing fine hair marks. Keep wiping off the brush so that any excess glaze is removed from the brush and not returned to the paint surface.

When the area is completed, remove the masking tape and allow the glaze to dry overnight. The result is the soft look of an unvarnished finish. If desired, a coat or two of satin varnish may be applied.

It is recommended that stippling is kept for the smaller areas of a room. One of the most difficult finishes to perform expertly is a stippled wall. Doors, skirting boards, architraves and cornices look wonderful stippled.

Dragging

The technique of dragging is perfect for doors, skirting boards and architraves. If working on such architectural timber, use a 50 mm cutting-in brush (house-painter's brush). A plain door can be transformed into a panelled piece, simply by masking out each panel, dragging and then moving on to the next section.

Oil-based glaze
❑ one part matt (flat) enamel
❑ one part scumble medium
❑ one to two parts turps
 (white spirit)

Water-based glaze
❑ two parts acrylic paint
❑ one part water scumble medium
Note: Don't use water unless the glaze is very thick

Tools
❑ roller to apply glaze
❑ wall-dragging brush (must have strong bristles)

Dragging requires two people working: one to apply the

glaze with a roller and the other to work up the ladder. Roll the glaze evenly onto the wall in strips about 900 mm wide. Roll the outside edge constantly so that the glaze doesn't get a dry edge – this shows as a darker stripe.

Jam the dragging brush into the glaze between the cornice and wall and then evenly drag down the wall. If you are on a ladder, just walk down the ladder without hesitating – hesitations will cause irregular stop-marks in the finish.

As you work down towards the skirting, feather the brush out, away from the wall. Wipe the brush, turn over to the other side, jam into the glaze at the skirting board and pull up the wall over the same area which you just dragged down.

Feather away from the wall near the cornice. This should be enough for good, strong drag marks. Continue around the room until each wall has been dragged.

1 Use a paint roller to roll the glaze on evenly

2 Jam the dragging brush into the glaze – as you work, feather the brush out away from the surface you are working on

Sponging

Low contrast is best for this finish – otherwise the room can look as though a demented animal has run across the walls! It is essential that you use real sea sponges as they impart a soft, subtle shape not possible with synthetic sponges.

Oil-based glaze
- ❏ one part matt (flat) enamel
- ❏ one part scumble medium
- ❏ one to two parts turps (white spirit)

Water-based glaze
- ❏ one part matt (flat) acrylic
- ❏ one part water scumble
- ❏ three parts or more water

Tools
- ❏ sea sponges
- ❏ 50 mm cutting-in brush
- ❏ round stipple brush

First, dip the sponges in water and wring out – this makes them soft and malleable. Load one sponge with the glaze

1 Load one sponge into the glaze and apply to the work surface in a random pattern

2 Dip a second sponge into turps (white spirit), or water if using a water-based glaze, and start to soften the first glaze, moving it around a little

and apply to the wall in a random pattern – working an area about 900 mm wide at a time from floor to ceiling.

Dip a second sponge into turps (white spirit), or water if using a water-based glaze, and start to soften the harsh edges of the glaze. Move the glaze around a little, taking some into the background space where there is no glaze at all. This creates a feeling of depth, and creates another tone.

Make sure that you work quickly and do not allow the glaze to dry up so that you have harsh join marks where you apply the next section.

You will find corners a little tricky and it is wise to use a cutting-in brush or a round stipple brush to help you get into the join. The last thing you want is a strong white line running down the corners of the room. If you think the finish is too strong, follow up with an overglaze (see page 43).

Parchment finish

This finish is best performed with the second glaze in oil-based paint and mediums. It requires two processes, but can be completed in one day. It gives a lovely, textured effect to the walls.

First glaze
- ❏ white acrylic paint – thick, straight out of the tin

Second glaze
- ❏ one part oil-based paint
- ❏ one part scumble medium
- ❏ one part turps (white spirit)

Tools
- ❏ 75 mm bristle brush
- ❏ washed lint-free cotton rags

Take the bristle brush and apply the first glaze to the wall in a random, slightly basket-weave pattern. Allow as many brushstrokes as possible to remain in the paint. Now take a rag which has been wrung out in water, and move the paint around slightly,

taking some into the previously untouched area. When you have finished, most of the wall should have varying areas of paint on it. There should be about 15 per cent only where the background is showing through. Allow to dry for one to two hours.

Take another rag and dip into the second glaze. Apply to the wall, patting on and rubbing, using a circular swirling motion. If you find you have applied too much glaze, or it is too dark, dip another cloth into turps (white spirit) and remove some.

When dry, this finish has texture and irregular areas of colour where the first glaze has sopped up the second glaze.

Make sure your application is reasonably even so that you do not have too much variation in the degree of colour.

Use parchment finish to give a lovely, textured effect to walls.

1 Apply the first glaze in a random, slightly basket-weave pattern, using the bristle brush

2 Move the paint around slightly, using a damp, wrung-out rag

3 Take another rag and apply the second glaze to the surface using a circular, swirling motion

Crackle finish

The furniture to be decorated must be prepared with as many coats of background colour in eggshell enamel (or eggshell acrylic) as are needed to be opaque. It is essential that the background is not porous and the background paint is absolutely dry before crackle medium is applied.

When ready to apply the crackle medium, first mask out the area with masking tape. This

1 First mask out the area with masking tape

2 Apply the crackle medium, allow to dry, cover with the paint then lightly mist with a fine water spray

3 Cut out the masking tape with a blade or you risk peeling the finish off

is necessary only if you intend to use the crackle medium as an inset. Once the tape is down (always run your thumbnail along the edge to ensure good bonding), apply the crackle medium. It is viscous and should be allowed to flow on rather than be painted on in the normal manner.

Make sure that the piece is horizontal, as the medium runs if on an angle and can create a mess. Allow the medium to dry, which can take from one to two hours to overnight, depending on the weather. Don't proceed to the next step until you are sure the medium is absolutely dry (it dries very flat and is often hard to see).

The paint used over the medium must be matt (flat) acrylic. You may use a household acrylic paint, but sometimes good quality artist's acrylics are even better. Often a deep tint base household paint will not crack so well because it is too heavily pigmented. You need to try your paint and medium on a sample board first.

If you want coarse, graphic cracking, use the paint straight out of the tin, with random brushstrokes. There must be no pressure on the brush. The loaded brush must glide over the medium. Keep reloading the brush. Cracking occurs in the direction of the brushstrokes.

If you want the fine, cobwebby cracking shown, thin the paint approximately two parts paint to one part water. Once you place the loaded brush, or roller for ease of application in this instance, on the dried crackle medium surface, it must merely glide over the surface and be reloaded constantly. Speed is of the essence. So, very quickly, apply the loaded brush to the surface, keep reloading and reapplying, using absolutely no pressure. Having applied all over, cover with the paint then lightly mist three to four times with a fine mist of water from a plant sprayer.

As the paint dries, which is almost immediately, the cracking occurs. If you wish to protect this finish, use oil-based or water-based varnish. Water-based varnish can reactivate the crackle medium, so be careful not to overwork it. However, once dry and matured for a few days, water-based paint is very strong and unless the piece of furniture receives a lot of wear, it is not essential to varnish.

A fabulous cracked, aged surface can be obtained on walls by using this medium. To be held satisfactorily on a vertical surface, the medium must be thinned one part crackle medium to one part water. It can then be painted onto a wall (must be non-porous) and will dry without running.

The big trick with this wall finish is that the acrylic paint which is used over the top of the medium must be thick, otherwise cracking will not occur over the thinned crackle medium.

Once the medium is absolutely dry, the acrylic paint may be applied. It looks best if random brushstrokes are used and, again, the brush must glide over the surface so that the crackle medium beneath is not disturbed. In this case, the paint should be applied with a brush, not a roller. Cracking usually occurs in the direction of the brushstrokes, so bear this in mind as you work. Don't forget to cut out the masking tape with a blade, or you will peel the finish off the wall.

A yellow wall that has been dragged

Varnishing

Varnish is the final coat that gives protection and an extra depth to painted finishes, depending on the number of coats applied. Of the many types of varnish available, gloss marine varnish offers the most protection – when matured and wet-sanded it has a smooth surface that withstands heat very well. Marine satin and matt (flat) varnishes are also hardy finishes, as are the old-fashioned resin-based varnishes.

Most varnishes tend to yellow slightly, but some can be deliberately tinted to correct this. Yellowing is fine over most colours except white and pale pastels. A little umber mixed in varnish to be applied over a red antiquing glaze gives an excellent result.

Surfaces which are used constantly require a great deal of protection and can be varnished in a number of ways, depending on the desired appearance. All varnishes, particularly high gloss, should be left to mature for a given time.

> When removing tape from crackle medium, it is essential that the tape is cut out with a blade or the entire finish will peel off with the tape.

Simple marbling for skirting boards

Skirting boards can become a very attractive, decorative feature in an otherwise simple or understated room.

Oil-based glaze
- ❑ one part matt (flat) enamel
- ❑ one part scumble medium
- ❑ one part turps (white spirit)

Water-based glaze
- ❑ one part matt (flat) acrylic
- ❑ one part water scumble
- ❑ one part water

Tools
- ❑ 50 mm cutting-in brush
- ❑ 50 mm round stipple brush
- ❑ feather
- ❑ newspaper

If you are working on a room 3 x 3 m you will need about forty pieces of tabloid newspaper. Fold each piece in half diagonally and then fold each side into a series of 25 mm concertinas. Paint the glaze onto the skirting board and quickly stipple to remove the brushstrokes. Now, with an up and down movement of the newspaper, break open the glaze to reveal the pale paint base beneath. Move the paper sideways on the glaze, thus creating fractures, leaving virtually none of the surface untouched. The trick with this finish is that all the surface has movement to it.

Make sure that the finish runs at a diagonal of about 45° – it must not be upright. As each piece of newspaper becomes clogged with glaze, discard. When the whole area is fractured, you can work over with a feather loaded with a little white glaze to add some veins. However, this finish will stand very well on its own without the application of veins.

With simple marbling, the colours should be very close together so that there is not too much overall contrast.

1 Paint the glaze on to the skirting board and quickly stipple to remove the brushstrokes

2 Using an up-and-down movement, use the newspaper to break open the glaze, revealing the pale paint base beneath

3 Work over fractured area with a feather loaded with a little white glaze to make a vein-like pattern

Blue walls with ragged insets and dragged main section

Colour recipes

Always combine a tiny amount first when mixing a colour and allow to dry before going ahead to mix in the desired quantity.

STONE:
- ❑ ten parts white
- ❑ five parts raw umber
- ❑ one part yellow ochre
- ❑ one part black

BLUE:
- ❑ ten parts white
- ❑ six parts blue
- ❑ one part orange
- ❑ one to two parts violet
- ❑ one to two parts raw umber

Painting a room is the cheapest way to redecorate, and it offers much more choice of colour schemes than wallpapering. It is also one of the most cost-effective DIY jobs, since almost all the expense of hiring a professional goes to pay for his or her time, whereas yours should be free.

INTERIOR PAINTING

Although paint is an economical finish, it doesn't have to look cheap. As well as allowing you to choose any colour scheme you can think of, it can be used on all the surfaces in a room so that the decorations complement one another, and it can also be used for a wide range of special effects.

To make colour-scheming even easier, most of the major manufacturers offer matched ranges that take away the guesswork of picking complementary shades. Each of these consists of a basic pastel colour, plus one or two toning paints that can be used to pick out details in the room. These all come in a range of different paint types that can be used on walls, woodwork and metalwork.

Even if you decide to go it alone, paint offers a lot more than the standard white for ceilings, a plain shade for the walls and white for all the woodwork that many people choose as the 'safe' option. Most standard paint ranges come in small 'tester' pots which are cheap to buy and allow you to try out different colour schemes at home, rather than guessing what they will look like. And you can even get paint mixed to your own requirements – to tone with existing tiles or flooring, perhaps.

The pictures opposite show a small range of the creative ideas which are possible using one or two different paint colours, and our section on colour scheming (see pages 10-21) shows you how to exploit some of the basic rules of colour to change the feel of a whole room. For example, you can make tall ceilings appear lower, small rooms appear airier, or throw more light into dark corners, simply by picking the right shade.

Finally, what about using paint to hide features which spoil the looks of a room, such as unsightly radiators, exposed pipework, uneven plasterwork? Painting eyesores the same colour as the background can help them to 'disappear', while a matt (flat) paint or 'broken colour' special effect finish can hide all sorts of irregularities in a surface.

Good organisation is the key to success, followed by the right preparation for the job at hand – a painted finish is only as good as the surface it covers.

1

Dulux

2

Dulux

3

Dulux

4

Interior colour schemes make the most of natural light if they are pale and warm. Pale tones will reflect light and make spaces look bigger. This will result in the need for less artificial light to achieve the same level of brightness. Choose a rich, creamy shade in preference to brilliant white as it will reflect a warmer glow. It is also much kinder to imperfect walls.

5

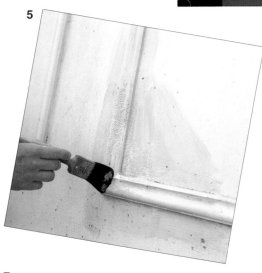

Paint is probably the least expensive and most effective way of bringing old rooms to life.

6

8

7

Dulux

Tools

A bad workman blames his tools, or so it's said – but choose the right ones and you won't have to make excuses for the finished results!

Painting tools have developed into a wide range of different brushes, rollers and pads, all of which are better for some situations than others, although a small range should cope with most household tasks.

Tools for walls and ceilings

The best option for large flat areas is to use a roller. This is quicker and easier than a brush, and also tends to spread the paint more evenly and economically. However, you may get more spatter, and the roller leaves a distinctive texture resembling orange peel, which will contrast with adjacent brushwork.

You still need to use a brush for finishing edges and awkward corners; a 50 mm brush will cope with most such areas,

although if you prefer pads to brushes, a small pad will do just as well. On small areas it is probably simpler to use a brush throughout. The ideal size for covering a large area quickly is a 100 mm brush, commonly called a wall brush. Although larger brushes are available, they are often tiring to use as their weight can be hard on the wrist muscles. Once again, paint pads are an alternative, and large pads are made specially for the job.

On very large areas, another option is to use a spray gun. Simple 'airless' guns can be bought quite cheaply, but better ones can be hired. Spraying applies the paint very quickly and evenly but is only worth considering where you are painting a large area in a single colour. It takes a long time to mask off all the areas you don't want painted, and the gun must be cleaned very thoroughly after use.

Tools for woodwork

Either brushes or pads can be used. This is as much a matter of personal preference as anything else. Although pads do tend to give a

more even finish, they are difficult to clean properly and can be tricky in awkward corners. Professionals sometimes use a small roller for large areas, but this is unlikely to be worthwhile in most houses. A 50 mm and 25 mm brush will cope with most jobs from windows to skirting boards and doors, although it may be useful to add a cutting-in brush for use on edges and corners. If you opt for pads, the most useful sizes are a 100 x 50 mm, plus a 50 x 50 mm and a crevice pad.

Tools for varnished wood

Varnish should always be applied with a brush; it's difficult to clean varnish out of a pad and the finish is not as good. Use the same size brushes as you would for applying paint, but keep a set specially for varnishing. If you use the same ones for paint you will find that it's almost impossible to clean them well enough to keep small flecks of dried paint out of the bristles, which will inevitably end up on the finished surface.

Choosing brushes

Good quality brushes have a thick filling of long, fine bristles which taper slightly to a point rather than spreading out. When buying a wall brush, don't choose one with coarse bristles – these are designed for applying masonry paint to exterior surfaces where the roughness would wear out a finer brush very quickly.

Cutting-in brushes have their bristles trimmed at an angle. The point this forms can very easily be run along an edge so you get a neat finish on things like window frames or internal angles.

> **TRICKS OF THE TRADE**
> New brushes always shed a few bristles, no matter how well made they are. Flex any new brush firmly across your hand a few times before use, to tease out any loose bristles.

Choosing rollers

Rollers can be fitted with different sleeves depending on what sort of paint you are using. The most expensive is lambswool, which holds the most paint, but cannot be used with oil-based paint. Mohair and synthetic pile can be used with oil- or water-based paint and are cheaper. Cheapest of all is plastic foam but this usually gives a poor finish and can spatter badly.

Standard roller sizes are 180 mm and 230 mm wide, but trade suppliers may stock rollers measuring 360 or even 460 mm, as well as narrow 50 mm rollers. You need a tray to match the width of the roller; if you buy roller paint in its own tray, this is intended for rollers up to 230 mm.

Most rollers can be fitted with an extension handle for use on ceilings. This usually simply pushes into a hollow socket in the handle.

Choosing paint pads

Pads are made from synthetic fibre or mohair pile backed with foam and bonded to a plastic or metal handle. Care must be used when loading them with paint since only the bristles should be filled. If the foam is allowed to become clogged with part-dried paint, the pad will not work properly. For this reason, you can buy special pad trays fitted with a roller to help pick up just the right amount of paint.

Other useful tools

Paint shields and paint kettles are cheap and well worth buying. A paint shield (or splatter shield if using a roller) can be held against an adjacent surface to prevent paint from getting on it when working up to an edge. A paint kettle allows you to decant a manageable amount of paint from a large tin, and helps to control the amount of paint that gets on the brush.

1-4 Selection of brushes
5 25 mm cutting-in brush
6 50 mm angled radiator brush
7-10 Selection of stripping knives
11 Combination shavehook
12 Paint pad
13 Paint pad edger
14 Scraper
15-18 Selection of roller brushes: mohair, lambswool and fibre
19 Paint tray
20 Rubber gloves
21 Blowtorch
22 Selection of sandpapers
23 Sandpaper block
24 Scraper
25 Face mask
26 Steel brush
27 Gloves
28 Steel wool
29 Orbital sander
30 Hot air gun

Cleaning tools

Good quality tools will be ruined unless they are cleaned carefully after every use – and even cheap, disposable tools will benefit from thorough cleaning. Brush restorer works well at shifting the stubborn deposits that result if paint gets into the bristles near the ferrule but is no magic solution when a brush has been badly neglected.

Work as much paint as possible out of brushes, rollers or pads by squeezing or scraping it out carefully, then brush off the surplus on several sheets of newspaper. Remove the rest with a suitable solvent.

❑ **Water-based emulsion.** Use lukewarm water with a small amount of washing up liquid. Work the bristles or pile carefully between your fingers to shift partially dried paint. Rinse in plenty of cold water until it runs clear. Flick the brush hard to drive water out of the base of the bristles, then pat dry with plenty of newspaper.

❑ **Water-based gloss.** This is easier to shift if you work washing up liquid into the bristles first. Then clean as for emulsion.

❑ **Oil-based gloss, eggshell and primer.** To clean brushes, half-fill a jar with turps (white spirit) or brush cleaner. Work the bristles up and down to ensure they are thoroughly soaked. To clean rollers or pads, pour the solvent into the tray and work the pile back and forth in it. If you used turps (white spirit), work washing up liquid into the bristles or pile, then wash thoroughly. If you used water-soluble brush cleaner, wash in lukewarm water and washing up liquid.

Store brushes by hanging them up (drill a hole in the handle if there isn't one already). Wrap the bristles in absorbent kitchen paper, folded over and secured with an elastic band. Remove a roller sleeve and hang the frame up by the handle. When the sleeve is thoroughly dry, store it in a plastic bag.

18

Preparation

Although there's always a temptation to slap the paint straight on – resist it at all costs. Modern paints make thorough preparation less vital than it once was, but no paint can hide a surface which is in poor condition. Time spent clearing up and masking off will ensure that the job runs smoothly and you get the results you want.

Planning the job

It's impossible to give an accurate timetable for every job, since so much depends on the situation and what you intend to do. However, it's easy enough for you to work out what's involved if you take the trouble to plan it in advance. But remember, the main cost of a decorating job is the labour. So although you stand to save a lot of money by doing it yourself, don't expect to redecorate a room from scratch in a day or two – although a lot can be done in advance in odd bits of spare time.

What's involved

The following checklist is a reminder of things to think about and the order in which to do them. They won't all be necessary in every case.

Step 1: Inspect for problems
Allow half an hour for a thorough check of the ceiling, walls, windows, door, fireplace or radiator, mouldings and fittings to make sure that no repairs are needed before decorating. Now is also the time to think whether there are any improvements you want to carry out – any built-in furniture or improved lighting? If you find anything that needs doing, get it repaired or sort it out yourself before going on. Look very carefully for any structural problems such as cracked ceilings, damp patches or rotten woodwork. And in old houses make sure that painted surfaces are stable – old distemper must be stripped before repainting.

Step 2: Go shopping
Plan your colour scheme and choose your finishes. Make a detailed shopping list of all the items and quantities required and arrange to buy or borrow any tools you don't already possess. If your survey showed up any special problems, buy whatever you need to put them right.

Step 3: Clear the room
Shift all the furniture you can into another room, and move the rest to the centre of the room. Remove fixtures if you can, otherwise mask them with tape and paper. Lift fitted carpets if possible, or cover them carefully with drop sheets taped down around the edges.

Step 4: Strip old decorations
Vacuum clean the whole room and take off old, unwanted fittings such as draught-proofing strips, panelling and so on. Strip old paint or unwanted paper from the ceiling. Strip old wallcoverings from the walls. Strip or sand woodwork.

Step 5: Make improvements
Install any new fixtures or fittings.

Step 6: Make good
Repair any damaged walls or ceilings. Fill and sand woodwork.

Step 7: Clean up
Vacuum up any dust. Wipe down ceiling, walls and woodwork with sugar soap and allow to dry. Ensure all drop sheets are in place.

Step 8: Apply any surface treatments
Hang lining paper if required. Prime woodwork, seal masonry surfaces and allow to dry.

Step 9: Apply topcoats
Work in this order: ceiling, walls, woodwork. Allow to dry thoroughly.

Step 10: Refit fixtures
Put back anything you removed and remove temporary masking.

Step 11: Clear up
Shift out all your tools and materials, remove drop sheets. Relay floorcoverings and replace furniture.

Patching chips, cracks and dents

Inspect cracks carefully to see whether there is any movement. Strengthen a joint if necessary; where movement is likely, fill with a flexible filler or aerosol foam to prevent it working loose.

❏ Fill large holes with general-purpose filler – either ready-mixed or powder type. Sand surrounding paintwork, rake out loose material and undercut so the filler can get a good grip. Where the hole is too big to support the filler, fill first with wadded newspaper or aerosol foam filler, then finish off with general-purpose filler. Sand when dry.

❏ For small cracks, fine-surface filler gives a better finish and bonds more firmly.

❏ Vulnerable corners can be filled with epoxy resin filler.

Lining the surface

When the wall is in very poor condition, lining paper provides a simple way to improve the surface. Hang it using much the same techniques as for wallpaper (see page 30 for full details). However, there are a few special points to watch.

Lining paper is much easier to hang than wallpaper, since it is light, needs no soaking and doesn't have a pattern to match. Hang it in vertical strips – the alternative technique of hanging it horizontally is only used when you are papering over it.

SURFACE

WALLS AND CEILINGS

Old wallpaper

Sound paint

Flaking paint

Paint-on lining paper

Distemper

Texture paint

Bare plasterboard

Bare plaster

New plaster

Bare brick

Indelible stains

WOODWORK AND FITTINGS

Sound paint

Flaking paint

Knots showing through paint

Bare iron and steel

Rusty iron and steel

Bare aluminium, copper, brass

In general it is best to strip. You may be able to paint successfully if the paper is sound, but there is always a risk of the pattern showing through. Most vinyl wallcoverings are unsuitable for painting. See page 29 for details of stripping wallpaper.

Sand down bumps and fill hollows. Wash down.

Scrape and sand back to sound paint. Fill patches with fine surface filler. Sand and wash down. If surface is very poor, hang lining paper.

If basically sound, stick down any lifting edges with wallpaper overlap/repair adhesive. Wipe down lightly with a damp cloth. If in bad condition, strip as for wallpaper.

Wash off by scrubbing with water.

Avoid stripping if possible; paint over it. If you have to strip apply texture paint remover to a small area at a time and scrape away when soft.

On new board, cover joints between boards with scrim tape and plaster. Paint nail heads with primer. Fill holes, cracks and dents and sand smooth. Wipe down with damp cloth.

Fill any blemishes and sand smooth. Wash down. If general condition is poor, hang lining paper, otherwise seal blemishes with primer/sealer.

Leave to dry for at least one month. Brush off any deposits and paint with emulsion paint; do not use an oil-based paint until new plaster is at least 6 months old.

Brush clean with a wire brush or stiff bristle brush. Coat with primer/sealer.

Water marks left on ceilings after a leak, nicotine stains and other marks may bleed through the paint. Cover with a special-purpose sealer or aerosol stain blocker.

Rub down minor blemishes and runs with medium glasspaper on a sanding block. Rub down the whole surface with fine glasspaper or a wad of steel wool to help the new paint to grip. Wash down with sugar soap and water to remove dust and grease.

If extensive, strip using heat or chemical stripper, or sand and scrape off. Small patches can be scraped back to sound paint and filled with fine surface filler.

Sand back to bare wood and apply shellac knotting compound .

Degrease with turps (white spirit). Rub down with steel wool or wet-and-dry paper. Prime immediately with oil-based general-purpose or metal primer.

Remove loose rust with a wire brush. Sand to bare metal with wet-and-dry paper or a flap wheel or treat with rust remover. Wash and dry quickly, then prime with oil-based metal primer.

No primer is needed, simply clean and key the surface with a non-metallic scouring pad.

Preparation tools

Filling prior to sanding and sealing

❏ **Scraping knife**: This has a broad flat blade which is stiff enough not to flex in use. Don't confuse it with a filling knife which is flexible. Different widths are available for large and small areas.

❏ **Shavehook**: This will scrape paint from mouldings and awkward areas. There are different shapes for flat and curved areas – a combination shavehook is most useful for general work as it will cope with almost any shape.

❏ **Sanding block**: Essential for hand sanding as it enables even pressure to be applied. Use with glasspaper in a range of grades for wood, or silicon carbide (wet-and-dry) paper for metalwork. A foam sanding block backed with abrasive will follow the contours of moulding.

❏ **Steel wool**: Comes in a range of grades and is very useful for sanding mouldings and awkward shapes.

❏ **Electric sander**: Sanding discs for electric drills are cheap and simple but don't give a very good finish. An orbital sander is better for large areas.

❏ **Wire brush**: Useful for removing flaking material or scratching a surface to help the paint to stick.

❏ **Filling knife**: Has a thin, flexible blade for filling flat areas.

❏ **Putty knife**: Handy for filling mouldings as the point and curve can be worked into awkward corners.

❏ **Blowtorch**: Useful for heat-stripping large areas of woodwork when used with a flame-spreader attachment.

❏ **Hot air gun**: Easier to control than a blowtorch and there is no risk of scorching the wood, although the heat can crack glass. Use with a heat-spreader attachment in confined areas.

❏ **Safety equipment**: Face mask and goggles to protect you from dust while sanding. Heavy-duty rubber gloves (industrial type) to protect you from paint stripper, or work gloves to protect your hands when heat stripping.

❏ **Useful bits and pieces**: A scrappy old paintbrush is still useful for applying stripper, and an old toothbrush is handy for odd corners. An old chisel is handy for scraping difficult corners and an old plastic card is perfect for applying filler to curves as it can be bent in your fingers.

Skill class
Paint stripping

Stripping is sometimes the only way to ensure that the new finish goes on easily and stays there. But it isn't always the best option, so weigh up the pros and cons carefully before you attack the existing surface.

Walls and ceilings

Walls and ceilings are rarely so bad as to need stripping completely. Badly flaking patches can be scraped off and filled, and powdery paint can be bound using sealer or stabilising solution. Alternatively, lining paper can be used to cover up the surface completely, although this should never be done unless it is stable. However, there are two cases in which stripping is the best solution – distemper and texture paint.

❏ **Distemper** is a very old form of finish used before emulsion paint was available. It is easily identified by rubbing your hand over the surface, which will feel chalky and leave a white deposit on your skin. Being basically a mixture of water-soluble glue and powdered chalk, distemper cannot be painted or papered over – since this destroys the bond between it and the underlying surface so that it simply falls off, taking the new finish

with it. The only answer is to remove it completely.

Start by brushing off all loose material, using a stiff brush and a vacuum cleaner to keep down the dust. Then wash off all remaining distemper with a bucket of water containing a little wallpaper stripper, a stiff brush and a cloth. Cover a small section at a time and change the water frequently. When dry, secure the surface by coating with primer/sealer or stabilising solution.

❏ **Texture paint** is always bad news if you don't like the finish. It was often applied to disguise defects in the plaster, although it may also have been done simply for effect. If it is covering poor plaster, you may be involved in extensive repair work once it has been removed, so check the condition of the underlying surface as much as you can before proceeding – on a ceiling the simplest option may be to lift a floorboard in the room above to see what state the ceiling plaster is in.

If you decide to go ahead, you will be in for some hard, messy work, as well as a fair amount of expense for the chemical texture paint remover that will be needed – it covers about 12 sq m per litre. Working on a small area at a time, paint this on, ensuring that the surface is well coated. Leave as instructed, usually about an

hour, then scrape away the softened paint for disposal. More than one treatment may be required. Finally, scrub the surface with coarse steel wool and soapy water.

Woodwork

When old paint is flaking or blistered, it's generally better to strip it all off and start again than risk defects occurring again after you have repainted. Stripping is also worth doing where successive layers of paint have built up to such a level that they have caused windows and doors to stick or filled in the fine detail of mouldings. And finally, if you want to varnish the woodwork, there is no alternative to stripping off the old paint and carefully cleaning the bare wood first. There are several options:

❏ **Scraping and sanding** is a cheap method, but very hard work on a large area unless the paint is badly flaking already. Sanding can create a lot of dust and can damage the form of a moulding, while scraping can leave scratches.

❏ **Heat** applied with either a blowtorch or a hot air gun is quite a cheap way to soften the paint so that it can be scraped away. But blowtorches can scorch the wood, leaving marks

which will be visible under varnish and must be covered to prevent them showing through paint. Heat is also difficult to use on windows as there is always a risk that it will crack the glass.

❏ **Chemical strippers** are expensive and make a lot of mess. But they are very good for mouldings, where the surface must not be damaged. You will also need solvent to clean off the residue and neutralise the stripper before applying the paint. Some types are water-soluble, while others need turps (white spirit). Although water-based types are easier to clean, the moisture does tend to raise the grain of the woodwork, which must be sanded when dry.

❏ **Dipping** is a form of chemical stripping carried out by immersing the wood in a bath of stripping agent. It can only be used on removable items like doors, but can be fairly economical compared to stripping by hand. However, the chemicals used do tend to remove the natural oils from the wood, leaving it looking rather dull and lifeless, while the moisture can loosen the joints. Local dipping firms can be found by looking in the Yellow Pages and most will collect and deliver bulky items like doors.

Heat stripping

Whether you use a blowtorch or a hot air gun, hold it in your left hand if you are right-handed and hold a stripping knife in your right. Wear a work glove on the hand holding the knife as any shreds which fall on you may be hot enough to burn. Protect the area beneath you with plenty of **wet** newspaper and have a metal container near to hand to catch the scrapings. Move the stripper back and forth across a small area of paint until it starts to bubble, then ease the blade of the knife under it. Work across the area like this, keeping the heat source slightly ahead of the knife and periodically discarding the shreds of paint. On awkward areas, hot air strippers can be fitted with a directional nozzle to prevent

Using a hot air gun

Painting on liquid stripper

Scraping off paint

heat from going where it isn't wanted.

If you are using a blowtorch, there is always a risk of scorching. If there are any visible burnt patches on the surface, they should be sanded smooth and primed using oil-based aluminium wood primer to avoid marks being left which could show through.

SAFETY TIP

When using a blowtorch there is a risk that shreds of paint or even the wood itself may catch alight. Always use wet newspaper instead of drop sheets, and have some means close to hand of putting out any accidental fires. Flame stripping is also risky when working on hollow panelling like that sometimes found on boxed or shuttered sash windows. Here the risk is that these areas contain sawdust and shavings which can easily take light and smoulder unnoticed. Check that this hasn't happened before you leave the room unattended.

Chemical stripping

The main choice is between liquid (or gel) stripper and paste stripper. Liquid is more economical, but may run off vertical surfaces and can need several applications where there are many layers of paint. With both types, protect your eyes with goggles and your hands with heavy rubber gloves and take care not to splash liquid stripper on you. Wash off accidental spills immediately and if you get any into your eyes, wash at once with plenty of water and seek medical advice.

Brush liquid stripper onto the surface and allow it to react with the paint. If there are several layers, you can speed its penetration by scoring the paint lightly first. Test a small patch periodically to see whether the stripper is through to the wood – don't try to remove it too soon. When the paint is thoroughly softened, scrape it away with a stripping knife or shavehook, taking care not to scratch the underlying surface. Deposit the scrapings as you go, ready for later disposal.

Butter paste stripper onto the surface with a knife, following the makers' instructions. Cover with plastic to avoid it drying out too quickly and leave time for the stripper to work through the paint. You can lift a corner of the plastic periodically to check whether the paint is thoroughly loosened, which may take several hours.

When the stripper has finished its job, peel away the plastic, which should remove most of the stripper and much of the paint. Then scrape away any remnants, disposing of them carefully. A second application should not be necessary.

After chemical stripping, neutralise and clean the surface with the recommended solvent, usually water or turps (white spirit). When dry, sand smooth.

Problem surfaces

❑ Plastic cannot be heat-stripped or chemical-stripped, since both techniques will damage the material. If paint is flaking it should lift off easily, otherwise leave and paint over.
❑ Aluminium should not be stripped with chemicals as they may react.

SAFETY TIP

Very old finishes may well contain lead, which is hazardous if swallowed or breathed in, particularly by young children. Old paint which might be chewed by babies is best stripped completely and repainted with a modern alternative which contains no lead.

Always be very careful when stripping old paint:
❑ Avoid sanding or dry stripping if possible as this creates hazardous dust – use chemicals or heat instead. Wear a mask if there is any dust, to prevent breathing it in, and vacuum it up as you go.
❑ Wrap up all flakes and shards of paint as soon as you have finished and dispose of them immediately.

❑ Iron fireplaces and windows cannot be heat-stripped. Use chemical stripper.
❑ Marble (e.g. fire surrounds) cannot be heat-stripped and chemicals may damage the surface polish, meaning that refinishing is required.

Ready to paint

Different surfaces and different finishes require more than one kind of paint, each of which has its own pros and cons.

Emulsion

This is the normal choice for walls and ceilings. All emulsions are water-based and usually contain vinyl; the paint dries by evaporation with little smell and is usually touch-dry in a couple of hours – a second coat can be applied after around four hours. Brushes can be cleaned in water. There are three different types of finish:

❏ **Matt (flat) emulsion** has no appreciable sheen and is best at hiding surface imperfections. It marks more than the other types but can be scrubbed clean.

❏ **Silk emulsion** has a soft sheen and a smoother surface that wipes clean more easily than matt (flat). It is good for surfaces that may get splashed or dirty, such as in kitchens and bathrooms.

❏ **Satin emulsion** is even shinier and is resistant to steam. Be careful when buying, though, as the term 'satin' is also used for some brands of eggshell paint, which is oil-based.

As well as the traditional liquid paint, emulsion also comes in thicker consistencies which are slightly more expensive but less prone to spatter.

❏ **Non-drip** paint has a jelly-like consistency which flows smoothly when brushed on. It is less prone to drip, although lumps can be dropped if too much is applied to the brush or roller.

❏ **Solid emulsion** (also called roller paint), is the consistency of butter and is sold in its own tray for use with a paint roller. It is even less likely to spatter, making it an excellent choice for ceilings.

❏ So-called **one-coat emulsion** is a special formulation which is designed to give good covering power when you are changing colour radically, such as when

paint in strips moving away from main light source

putting a light colour over a dark one. In such circumstances it is well worth using.

Eggshell

Eggshell is an alternative to emulsion for walls and ceilings, but can also be used on wood and metal. It is oil-based, so takes longer to dry than emulsion and has a strong smell. It is normally touch-dry in 4-6 hours and can be repainted after about 16 hours.

Eggshell has good covering power and gives a tough sheen that is easy to keep clean. When used on walls, it can be applied directly to the surface, although a primer and an undercoat may be needed on other materials. It should not be used over new lining paper unless this is primed first, as the paper tends to absorb the solvent.

Turps (white spirit) or brush cleaner must be used for cleaning painting tools and mopping up drips.

Gloss

Gloss is the most common choice for woodwork and fittings, although it can be used on walls, too. When used on walls, it gives a tough, water-resistant finish, but any bumps, hollows or cracks will be more obvious.

Both water-based and oil-based types are available. Either can be used on plaster and woodwork, although iron

Kitchen-dining area with natural timber ceiling and floor and painted interior with mauve trims

Dulux

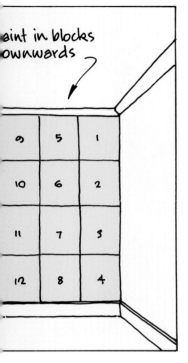

aint in blocks
ownwards

9	5	1
10	6	2
11	7	3
12	8	4

and steel should only be painted with oil-based paints. A suitable primer and undercoat are normally needed, depending on the material being painted.

❏ **Oil-based gloss** takes around 4-6 hours to dry and around 16 hours before a second coat can be applied. Tools must be cleaned with turps (white spirit) or brush cleaner.

❏ **Water-based gloss** (such as acrylic gloss) dries quickly with little smell in an hour or two, and can be recoated the same day.

> **TRICKS OF THE TRADE**
> Water-based gloss can be used on wood which has been washed down, without having to wait for it to dry thoroughly – handy when time is short.

❏ **Microporous paints** are water-based and designed to allow the wood to breathe through the finish. Their special properties are handy outdoors, but should not be necessary inside.

This light-filled family room is made warm and friendly by a yellow interior with white trims

Enamel

Enamel paints are high-quality gloss finishes which build up a very tough surface. They are good for smaller jobs and difficult surfaces, but tend to be expensive. Special types include rust-resistant enamel which can be used on metal without primer or undercoat, heat-resistant enamel designed to resist discoloration on pipes and radiators and bath and porcelain enamel for repairing plumbing fittings. Many enamels can also be bought in spray cans which are convenient for items such as furniture. Special solvents may be needed for cleaning painting tools and in some cases the manufacturers will advise special surface treatment or application methods for the best results.

Undercoat

Undercoat serves two purposes. It contains a lot of solid material which builds up very quickly to fill surface imperfections, improving the final finish, while its dense colour means that the topcoat does not need to conceal any underlying paint. It should always be bought as recommended by the makers of the topcoat, as this ensures that both its formulation and colour will be compatible. Oil-based undercoat will require turps (white spirit) or brush cleaner.

> **TRICKS OF THE TRADE**
> All paints used for children's rooms or furniture must be lead-free. Most modern paints contain no lead, and will say so on the tin – the only ones likely to cause a problem are certain types of primer, such as calcium plumbate and red lead.

Primers and sealers

Primers are designed to bond with the surface to which the paint is being applied and provide a good basis for subsequent coats. They come in a wide range of different formulations to be used depending on the material you are painting.

Sealers are used on masonry and wood to bind an unstable surface or prevent any chemicals the material contains from affecting the surface finish.

The most useful primers and sealers are general-purpose and have several applications, although you may still need special ones for unusual materials. **Acrylic primer** is a water-based general-purpose preparation which dries very quickly and can be used for wood, plasterboard and masonry. It should not be used on ironwork as it can cause corrosion, so nail heads in woodwork may cause problems unless painted with an oil-based primer first. Some types have similar properties to an undercoat and are sold as primer/undercoat.

General-purpose or **Universal primer** is an oil-based coating suitable for wood and most metals, although it may not work as well as specialised primers on some metals. It dries in about six hours.

Primer sealer is an oil-based coating for plaster and porous or powdery surfaces. Allow a day to dry.

Dulux

Loading up a brush with paint

Brushing paint on correctly in vertical strips

Basic techniques

Mastering the basic skills of painting with a brush or roller will guarantee a better finish and less effort on your part.

The first thing to do is to read the label, then open the paint tin carefully. Wipe the lid with a cloth to remove any dust or dirt and prise it open trying to avoid damaging it. Most people prise with a screwdriver, but this tends to bend the lid, making it hard to reseal. A better tool which should be to hand is the side of a wide-bladed scraper.

Unless the makers specifically advise against it, stir the paint in the tin thoroughly, using a clean stick, then decant it for use, depending on whether you are using a brush, roller or pad.

Brush painting

Most people start by painting straight from the tin, but it's better to get into the habit of using a paint kettle.
The advantages are that this prevents the paint in the tin from drying or becoming contaminated, while the kettle has a more convenient handle, and room to insert the brush easily, and can be

refilled so it always holds the ideal quantity of paint. Fill the kettle about one-third to half full and tie a length of string tightly across the handle to act as a brush rest and scraper.

Tease any loose bristles or dust out of the brush and then dip it into the paint no more than about one-third of the length of the bristles. This prevents paint from getting into the ferrule – very important as it is hard to clean out properly and causes the bristles to stiffen. Scrape off excess paint against the string on the kettle as you draw it out.

When using a medium or large brush, grip it in your fist, as it is tiring to hold in your fingers. Always apply the paint so that you brush away from the wet edge rather than into it, so that the paint thins out across the unpainted surface. This technique, called 'feathering', ensures that no ridges form between areas of paint. On large areas, the basic technique is to apply the paint in vertical bands – helping to prevent runs. Brush several adjoining strips until the paint on the brush starts to run out, then lightly brush across in

horizontal strokes to level off the surface. Finish off with very light vertical strokes, then reload the brush and continue from the edge of the patch.

On small areas, modify the basic technique. Hold a small brush like a pen and fill in with light strokes. Lift off when the paint starts to run out and smooth off with one continuous stroke.

Roller painting

Fit a roller sleeve to suit the paint, then decant the paint into a roller tray, taking care not to overfill it. It's important not to cover the angled ramp as this is used to distribute the paint evenly over the rollers.

Load the roller carefully; to avoid getting too much paint on the sleeve only dip the pile lightly into the paint and then roll on the ramp several times to spread it. Covering an area of about half a square metre, roll the paint onto the surface in a series of interlocking strokes. When using water-based paint it is easiest to use horizontal, criss-cross strokes, but with oil-based paint it is better to use vertical zigzags as this makes runs less likely. Continue until the roller

Applying paint horizontally

Using a roller brush to apply paint on the diagonal

begins to empty. Then roll across the whole area with parallel strokes to fill in and even out the paint.

Using pads

Decant the paint into a pad tray or roller tray. Dip the pad lightly into the surface or run it across the loading roller to avoid getting paint on the backing foam. Then apply the paint to the surface with a series of short, interlocking strokes. Cover an area of no more than a square metre at a time, then go back and lightly sweep over any marks.

Order of painting

The order in which you paint different parts of the room is important as it ensures that you don't spatter paint on freshly decorated areas, and don't have to stop at an inconvenient spot.

To minimise problems with drips, the general rule is to start at the top and work downwards – so paint the ceiling first, then the walls. If there is a coving, cornice or ceiling moulding, paint it at the same time as the ceiling if you want it the same colour – otherwise paint it after the ceiling and before the walls.

Paint all of a given area (such as the whole ceiling or the whole of one wall) in one go without stopping, as even a short break can leave visible marks where patches have dried before continuing to paint. If you are working with a partner, don't both try to work on the same area at once, but each do separate walls and aim to complete them in one go.

A second general rule is to start at the window and paint away from the light, as this makes it easier to see the area you have painted. Where there is more than one window, start at the largest or brightest source of light. On window walls and walls opposite the source of light, just work from right to left if you are left-handed, left to right if you are right-handed.

How much paint?

Make sure you buy enough paint to finish the job in one go. If you have to buy extra, you may find that the colour is not a good match, particularly when the shade was mixed specially.

There are no hard and fast rules about how much paint you will need. Although most makers list the coverage of their paint on the tin,

these figures can only be an approximate guide, as the state of the surface affects how much paint is absorbed and how far it will go. Very absorbent or heavily textured surfaces need more paint than smooth ones, and if you are making a drastic colour change you may also need more than normal to hide the basecoat. Non-drip, one-coat and 'solid' paints tend to cover a smaller area, but need fewer coats. Finally, paint tends to go further when the weather is cold and damp than when it is warm and dry.

As a very rough guide, the maximum area that one litre of emulsion or eggshell will cover is about 16 sq m. The minimum is around 12 sq m, depending on brand. Undercoat covers from about 12-14 sq m and gloss can vary from as little as 10 to as much as 17 sq m.

To calculate the area you have to deal with, measure the length and width of the room and the height of the ceiling (all in metres). To get the total wall area, add the length to the width, multiply by the height and multiply by two. Unless you have huge picture windows, any glazed area can safely be ignored since it's as well to have a

little more paint than you need. To get the total ceiling area, multiply the length by the width.

The area of the woodwork is harder to calculate, although each side of a standard door is about 2 sq m. Skirting boards, door frames and window frames are normally about 0.1 to 0.15 sq m for every metre of their length, but here it is especially important to err on the side of generosity as mouldings tend to use much more paint than flat areas.

Finally, don't forget that the areas you have calculated only allow for one coat, so double them where two coats will be needed.

TRICKS OF THE TRADE
It's not really a good idea to use old paint, since partial drying may have changed its properties, but sometimes it is unavoidable – for example if you are patching up an existing job using the original colour. If the old paint has formed a skin on the surface, you may be able to reclaim it by carefully cutting round the skin, lifting it out in one piece and discarding it. Strain the remaining paint through an old pair of tights to filter out particles.

Skill Class
Painting ceilings and walls

Painting ceilings

If you are using a roller, start by brushing a strip all round the edges of the ceiling and any light fittings, covering an area about 100 mm wide. Then switch to your roller, working away from the light source in strips about a metre wide. Keep the roller in front of you so any spatter does not fall on your head. You can either use a platform or fit the roller with an extension handle; although an extension roller is less easy to control, there is no need to watch your footing when working backwards.

On small ceilings you can do the whole job with a wall brush, although it is tiring on your arm. Be especially careful not to overload the brush, although in time paint is likely to work down the bristles however much you try to avoid it.

> **TRICKS OF THE TRADE**
> Although you can get brushes with drip shields, it's easy to make one to fit any ordinary brush. Punch a hole in a piece of card (or a paper plate) and slip it over the handle to catch drips.

Painting walls

As with ceilings, if you are using a roller you need to paint the edges and corners with a brush first. Remembering to work away from the light where relevant, start at the top and work down in strips about a metre wide, then move on to the next strip.

When you are intending to paint the woodwork as well, carry the paint over from the walls slightly onto skirting boards and door frames, so that the edge will be covered by the paint used on the woodwork. Not only is this easier than trying to paint up to the edge of the wood, but it helps to ensure that there are no unpainted gaps between the two areas.

When dealing with radiators you have two options. Either use a long-handled

An elegant sitting-dining room with a soft, whitish-green interior, a Carrara marble fireplace, white painted woodwork and a natural timber floor

radiator brush to reach as far down behind the radiator as you can, or arrange to release the radiator from its brackets and hinge it down onto the floor. Although the latter course may seem somewhat drastic, in practice it is usually fairly simple and can be done without draining the system, providing there is some play in the pipework, simply by slackening the joint nuts. Whether it is worth doing depends on where the radiator is and how visible the wall behind it is.

> **TRICKS OF THE TRADE**
> When painting fine details use a sign-writer's rest made from a piece of dowel padded at one end with lint-free cloth. Use the stick to form a rest for your wrist.

Cornices and mouldings

Plaster cornices and mouldings are attractive features that you may want to highlight by using a contrasting paint. Bearing in mind the general order of painting, it's simply a matter of taking care along the edges where the mouldings meet ceilings or walls.

On straight-edged mouldings, protect adjacent, finished surfaces with a paint shield, and define the edges of the moulding first using a 25 mm brush or cutting-in brush. To get a clean edge, twist the brush slightly against the surface so that a small bead of paint is squeezed out of the bristles. Draw this along the edge as if drawing a line with a pen.

Some mouldings have

Painted cornice

decorative edges which may overhang the adjacent surface. Slip the edge of the paint shield or a piece of stiff card under the edge to stop paint spattering the finished surface, then use a small brush to pick out the edge.

Fill in the remaining area with a 50 mm or 25 mm brush depending on the shapes. With complicated mouldings, try using a stippling action to get an even coating of paint.

Painting skirting boards and picture rails

Skirting boards

Skirting boards are much easier when there is no carpet, so release the edge and roll it back if possible. If you don't, it is virtually impossible to avoid getting some paint on the carpet and getting carpet fibres stuck in the paint.

Foam-backed carpets are stuck down with double-sided carpet tape and are virtually impossible to lift without damage. All you can do is cover them with drop sheets and tape along the edge. Hessian-backed carpets are normally held in place by grippers nailed to the floor just away from the skirting, although you may also find tacks. The professional tools for releasing a carpet held on grippers are a kneekicker and carpet-fitter's bolster, which can be hired. Alternatively, you can improvise using a bricklaying bolster (clean it up with wet-and-dry paper) and a home-made kneekicker (see Tricks of the Trade).

To use the kneekicker, kneel near the skirting and push the teeth of the kicker into the pile. Jerk it forward with your knee and pull upward to release the carpet from the grippers. Work the bolster in to free the edge. When you have released the edge completely, roll it back to clear the skirting. From now on, mind your fingers and knees when working on the skirting, as the grippers have very sharp teeth. To replace the carpet, use the kneekicker again, jerking the carpet forward over the gripper and using the bolster to

Dulux

work the backing down on to the gripper teeth.

Use a small brush or cutting-in brush to pick out the top edge of the skirting, then fill in the area below using a larger brush. Even when the carpet has been lifted, use a paint shield when you brush along the bottom of the skirting. Otherwise, you run the risk of picking up dust from the cracks below.

Picture rails

Picture rails (and other mouldings such as dados) are straightforward to paint, but need care because they are narrow and have a clearly visible edge. Rub down, vacuum-clean and wipe them thoroughly before you start as they can be real dust traps.

Start by using a small brush to pick out the edge – a cutting-in brush is often easier for this and a paint shield can prove a big help. Then run along with a larger brush to finish the rest of the moulding.

Painted skirting board

TIPSTRIP

TWO-COLOUR PAINT JOBS
If you are picking out details in a second colour, use a small artist's brush to fill in the details when the base coat is dry.

TRICKS OF THE TRADE

You can improvise a kneekicker from a slab of wood screwed to a short length of stout timber. Drive at least a dozen strong nails through the wood so that they project a short way – enough to get a good purchase on the carpet. Pad the opposite end of the timber with a thick wad of cloth or layers of carpet nailed in place.

Painting woodwork

The golden rule for all woodwork is to apply the paint evenly. It is always easier to put on a second coat than to get rid of drips and runs. Use the right size of brush for the job, a 50 mm brush for large areas and a 25 mm for small details and mouldings. Plan the work so you don't have to stop halfway, and always work up to a clearly defined edge or corner.

If possible start at the top and work down. Paint in long,

even strokes along the grain, blending each strip with the previous one. If you are painting to an edge, draw the brush off it with light pressure, otherwise the edge will act like a scraper, removing a large amount of paint and causing a run.

When the brush starts to run dry, 'lay off' with short, light strokes, then recharge the brush. Pick up in the area you laid off, blending the new stroke with the last. Never try to start in an area which has

partially dried, or the brush will drag on the surface leaving indelible marks.

If you are unfortunate enough to start a run, brush the paint out over the surface as quickly as it appears.

With decorative shapes, the basic rule is that the brush should follow the tool which made the shape. So, on mouldings work along in strips to ensure that you fill each curve evenly, and on turned woodwork, right round each change of shape one after another.

Painting doors

There is a set sequence for painting a door which ensures that the job is done in manageable sections and that you don't have to reach across areas which you have already done. The painting pattern varies according to whether you are dealing with a panelled or a flush door. Glazed doors can be painted as if you were dealing with a window.

Before you start, wedge the door ajar so you can reach all sides of it and get in and out easily. Then unscrew the door handles, lock covers, fingerplates and so on, but keep the handle nearby just in case someone shuts the door by mistake. Then rub down and wash the existing paintwork. Don't forget to clean the top of the door, always a real dust trap.

Panel door

Do the flat area of the panels first, working from top to bottom, left to right. As you complete each one switch to the small brush and run it along the mouldings, making sure you don't leave an excess of paint in the corners to start runs. Then paint the centre rails and stiles, starting at the top and working down. Next paint the outer stiles and edges of the door, taking care to lift the brush lightly as you draw it off the edges to avoid the risk of an excess of paint causing a run. Finally, paint the frame.

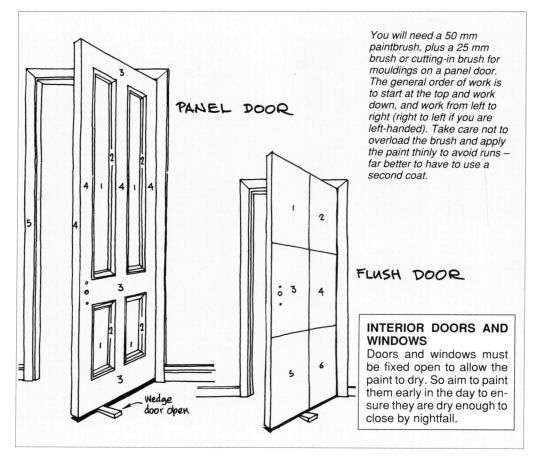

PANEL DOOR

FLUSH DOOR

Wedge door open

You will need a 50 mm paintbrush, plus a 25 mm brush or cutting-in brush for mouldings on a panel door. The general order of work is to start at the top and work down, and work from left to right (right to left if you are left-handed). Take care not to overload the brush and apply the paint thinly to avoid runs – far better to have to use a second coat.

> **INTERIOR DOORS AND WINDOWS**
> Doors and windows must be fixed open to allow the paint to dry. So aim to paint them early in the day to ensure they are dry enough to close by nightfall.

Panel door

Flush door

Work quickly using long, even strokes and don't over-brush. Divide the door into imaginary panels, two across and four down, and complete these one at a time before merging the edge into the next 'panel'. Next paint the edge of the door, taking care not to leave an excess on the corners. Finally, paint the frame.

Painting windows

Windows are fiddly to paint, especially if they have a lot of small panes. They also need special care in preparation, since even the inner faces suffer from the effects of the weather, which can cause frames to crack, paint to blister and putty to drop out. Repair any damage and make good all these blemishes before you start work, then rub down and wipe clean. Once again, it is a good idea to unscrew all fittings before you paint.

As with doors, there is a set painting sequence which ensures that you don't have to touch areas which have already been painted. This sequence varies depending on whether you are dealing with hinged casements or sliding sashes. Once again, the general rule is to start at the top and work down, and to work from left to right unless you are left-handed.

In order to stop water seeping in around the glass, the paint should be allowed to carry slightly over onto it – around 3 mm or so – to provide a weatherseal. There are two basic approaches to achieving this:
- Mask all round each pane by running masking tape about 3 mm away from the frame. This is effective but longwinded. Remove the tape before the paint is fully hard.
- Paint round the frame fairly carefully using a cutting-in brush or hand-held paint shield to ensure that you leave a weatherseal. Then when the paint is dry, trim off any surplus using a window scraper (good quality ones are designed to leave a small amount of paint on the glass as an even weatherseal around the frame).

Casement window

Fix the casement ajar with a temporary stay made from a stick or stiff wire. Then paint round each pane in turn, covering the glazing bars as you go. Next paint the top rail, fol-

Laura Ashley

Sash window in a kitchen

lowed by the bottom rail, the hinged side of the window, and the opening side of the window. Finally, paint the frame.

Sash window

These are more complicated as you cannot reach all parts of the window at once; the trick is to work in two sessions and to move the sashes over each other in the middle of the job. Take care to paint the sliding surfaces as thinly as you can; all too many sashes become glued immovably by an excess of paint.

❏ Open the window and slide the sashes right over one another, leaving a small gap at top and bottom. Do the outer sash first, starting with the underside and inside of the bottom rail. Then paint the stiles and glazing bars as far up as you can go. Now do the exposed part of the runners on the outer frame. Finally, on the inner sash, just paint the underside and inside of the bottom rail.

❏ Reverse the sashes and slide them nearly closed. Do the outer sash first, starting with the top rail, followed by the upper part of the glazing bars and stiles which you could not reach before. Now do the exposed area of the sash runners in the frame. Next complete the inner sash, top rail first, then glazing bars and stiles. Finally, paint the frame.

When the paint is touch-dry, move the sashes up and down to ensure that they are not sticking, and use a small brush to fill in any areas you missed.

Painting a staircase

Staircases must be painted very carefully if you are doing all the woodwork, simply because there is so much of it. And if you are intending to paint the treads, you must be able to ensure that no-one will walk on them until they are thoroughly dry – at least one day and preferably more. Life is much easier if you are only painting the handrail and balustrade, or if you are only painting the edges of the treads and running a carpet down the middle.

Lift any stair carpet and underlay pads first, and vacuum up the dust. Prepare the woodwork carefully, after fixing any loose parts of the handrail. Turned and moulded parts can be cleaned and rubbed down much more easily with a handful of steel wool than with glasspaper, then wiped down with a cloth moistened with a solution of sugar soap. Prepare the handrail carefully as it must present a very smooth surface to people's hands.

The general order of work is to start at the top and work downwards. The first golden rule is to plan the job so you don't stop in the middle of an area, and the second golden rule is to remember which bits can safely be touched.

Start by painting (or varnishing) the individual balusters or spindles. This is a slow job when these are a complicated turned shape, since each one must be brushed all round avoiding gaps, drips or runs – and there is no substitute for time when doing this. Don't paint the handrail yet, as you may need to lean over it in order to reach the opposite side of each baluster. Next paint (or varnish) the newel posts, starting at the top and working down. This is normally a much quicker job as there are more large flat areas.

Then paint the handrail. Do the flat part on the underside first as this is fiddly, working in between the balusters all the way down the rail. Then do the top of the rail in one go so you get a smooth, unbroken coat. The rail needs at least two coats and preferably more, because of the heavy wear it suffers. Rub down with fine glasspaper or steel wool between coats to ensure a really smooth surface.

Unless you have to complete the stairs in one go, now is a convenient place to take a break and allow the paint to dry since there is a fairly high risk of accidentally touching the balustrade.

If you are painting or varnishing the treads and risers, these come next. Start at the top and work down. If you are doing the whole width of the stairs, remember you will be trapped at the bottom (and anyone upstairs will be stuck there, too) until the paint is dry. If you are only doing a strip each side and carpeting the centre, this is not a problem, but it is still a good idea to leave the paint until touch-dry before continuing.

Last of all, paint the strings down each side of the staircase. The string along the wall side should be done first, followed by the inside of the outer string. The outer side of the outer string, as well as any panelling below it, can then be painted from a stepladder without needing to climb the stairs and risk touching the wet paint.

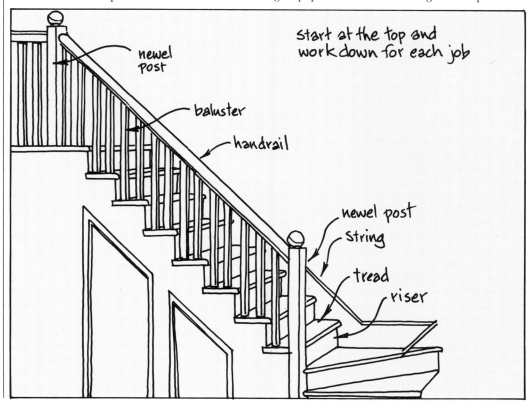

Whether you are painting a new or renovated home or repainting an existing one, the job of painting the exterior is a major task. But it's not as difficult as it looks – especially with a few tricks of the trade up your sleeve!

EXTERIOR PAINTING

If you choose to have the house painted by a team of professional painters, the cost could well be beyond your budget. There are a few tricks of the trade which can help you save a large proportion of the cost if you do it yourself.

In painting or repainting your home, different surfaces require different preparation and treatment. There are hundreds of products available, all specially designed for particular situations. Most of the new products and systems are at least equivalent to the existing products. Modern water-based acrylic paints are now available for most applications and are comparable in performance, and in some cases superior to, the more traditional solvent-based paints. The key to a successful painting project is proper planning and preparation. Any painting project will only be as good as the work done in preparing the surfaces prior to painting. If you skimp on the filling and the sanding, the blemishes will show through to the final coats. If you omit essential steps and fail to allow adequate drying times between coats, the surface will show it. In some cases, the use of inappropriate materials and finishes could cause the paint to peel off a short time after the job has been completed.

There is an accepted order of work in any major painting job. Generally, a professional painter will start at the top (gutters and fascias), and work down (eaves, walls, windows and doors), saving the small details until last. In this way any drips and spatters will be covered by the finishing coats on the way down and no completed surfaces will be damaged by the work following. The second benefit of working from the top down is that the easy work on the ground can be completed last, when you are tired!

Proper job planning also includes the correct choice of tools and equipment. Hiring an extension ladder or scaffold system can save considerable time and effort and make the job go more smoothly. The correct tools will reduce fatigue – an important factor when you are working up high on a ladder.

It's important to do your homework properly when it comes to selecting paint and other materials. Some paint systems are incompatible with others; some systems require special preparation following the manufacturer's instructions. It pays to shop around for a good deal and seek professional advice if you are unsure about what you need.

The key to a successful painting job is proper planning and preparation.

Porters Lime Wash

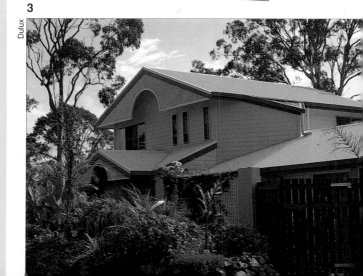

Dulux

1 An example of exterior pattern and texture
2 Terracotta lime-washed exterior
3 Latticework adds a textured facade to this two-colour painted exterior

4

4 This exterior shows four stages of restoration: paint has been burnt off the exterior (side, top left); the burnt paint has been scraped away (bottom left); the French doors have been primed

6

(bottom right); the French doors and front facade have been primed and sealed (top left and right)
5 Detail of facade where the paint has been burnt off
6 Detail of scraped facade

5

7

7 A new look can be as easy as repainting your front door (see pp.76-77)
8 Painted latticework
9 Spruce up your picket

fence with a new coat of paint
10 Give your windows a facelift (see p.76)
11 Lime-washed house

8

9

(see pp.76-77)
(see p.76)

GREEN TIP

When painting the outside of your home, consider the visual impact of your colour scheme. Try to make it blend sympathetically with the surroundings.

Use external colours to heat or cool your home naturally. Light-coloured walls will reflect sunlight and heat – dark-coloured walls will absorb them.

When it is time to repaint your home an easy tip like this will reduce your power bills considerably.

10

Always observe safety procedures, especially when working high up.

Dulux

11

Porters Lime Wash

65

Tools and equipment

There are good tools and there are cheap tools, but unfortunately there are very few good, cheap tools.

Painting the exterior of your home is a major task and the investment in quality tools and equipment will pay dividends. The average external painting job will require some or all of the following tools and equipment:

- ❏ 50 mm brushes
- ❏ 100 mm brushes
- ❏ cutting-in brush
- ❏ paint roller and roller tray
- ❏ paint kettle
- ❏ extension handles for roller
- ❏ masking tape
- ❏ drop sheets
- ❏ airless spray gun
- ❏ cleaning rags
- ❏ mineral turpentine (turps/white spirit)
- ❏ brush cleaner
- ❏ ladder plus stay and tool-tray or hook
- ❏ planks
- ❏ scaffold tower and boards
- ❏ glasspaper and wet-and-dry paper
- ❏ wire brush

Brushes

For painting masonry, brickwork and render, a 100 mm heavy-duty, trade quality brush is essential. The wear and tear on a brush is most severe when painting this type of surface and a strong bristle brush is necessary.

A smaller 50 mm brush and an angled, cutting-in brush are handy for painting timber and cutting in around windows and door frames. These sizes are also useful for gutters, downpipes and other areas where some precision is required.

Always use a new brush for varnishes and other clear finishes, and keep that brush exclusively for this purpose. Clear finishes tend to bleed paint residue from brushes, which may leave streaks in the finish.

Keep an extra couple of brushes handy when you are working up high to save climbing up and down the ladder. The advantage of a tool-tray is that a variety of paints and equipment can be kept close at hand.

Roller painting

For large areas of painting, nothing beats the roller for quick application. Select a roller according to the roughness of the surfaces to be painted. Painted brick and coarse render require a longer nap roller than smooth render. Extension handles are a tremendous advantage as you can reach higher while still working on the ground. Your paint supplier will be able to advise on the selection of rollers and extensions.

There are a number of roller tray styles on the market. Remember that when you are up on a ladder you won't want to climb up and down constantly refilling a small roller tray. Select a large trade-quality design that can be clipped to your ladder at a convenient height.

Airless spray guns

These spray guns are very useful for painting difficult materials like trellises and latticework. They work by electrically activated vibrating pistons which atomise the

Skill Class
Spray painting

Build up thicker coats with successive applications. Spraying too much paint in one pass will cause drips and runs.
❏ Use the gun in a crosswise motion, keeping it a uniform distance from the surface.
❏ Press the trigger only when the gun is moving and release it at the end of each stroke.
❏ Move the gun from left to right, pressing the trigger. Release the trigger near the completion of the stroke then stop the motion. Reverse the above action.

A small practice run on a waste piece of timber will help your rhythm. This method of spray painting will help prevent runs.

Accessories are available which allow you to use paint direct from the tin rather than the relatively small reservoirs supplied as standard.

paints. Make sure that you use the appropriate model as some designs may not be suitable for some water-based paints.

Follow the manufacturer's instructions for thinning and cleaning up.

Comprehensive and careful masking of adjacent areas will be required. Use these guns on calm days only,

to control overspray. Airless spray painting is very quick and gives good paint penetration even to porous and uneven surfaces.

Masking tape and protection

The worst part of painting is the cleaning up afterwards. Regardless of how carefully you work, some paint will inevitably drip onto glass and window frames. Precious plants and landscaping may be damaged by paint spatters and drips and, of course, paint spills can happen a lot more easily than you think!

It is essential to mask off all windows and door frames when painting. Masking tape and newspaper is generally sufficient, but special masking tools are also available and these can speed up the job considerably.

Use plenty of drop sheets to protect horizontal surfaces. You should also consider protecting your neighbour's property if it is likely that you will cause any damage.

Five minutes of protection is better than hours of cleaning up (or making up!).

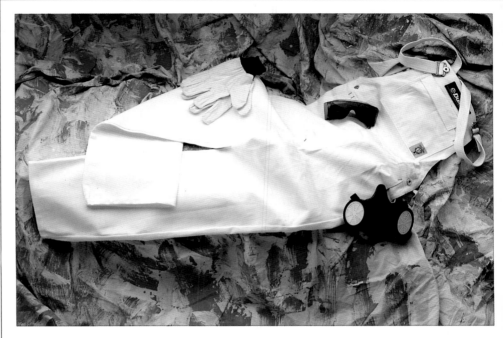

Protection

❏ Always use turps (white spirit), thinners or brush-cleaning fluids in a well-ventilated area.

❏ Don't smoke while painting or cleaning up – these chemicals are highly flammable. If in doubt, do the work out of doors, and never paint close to an exposed flame.

❏ Apart from the dangers of fire and possible explosion, these chemicals can also cause skin damage and irritation. When painting and cleaning up, gloves and eye protection should be worn. Lightweight gloves give good protection: the disposable plastic surgical gloves available from chemists are cheap and quite effective.

❏ When sanding timber and old paint, wear a paper dust mask to avoid inhaling the dust. A face mask with a special filter should be worn to reduce the amount of fumes inhaled while using oil-based paints and when using spray-painting equipment.

❏ Paint, especially solvent-based sealers and undercoats, can be very difficult to remove from skin and hair. Wear a hat when you are painting overhead, and protective spectacles or goggles.

❏ Use barrier creams to protect exposed skin. These creams prevent paint penetrating the skin and make removal much less difficult.

Good access

Easy, safe access to the work area is always important when painting, but particularly when painting at different heights, starting from the top and working down.

Ladders

A stepladder is almost essential equipment for any home. Few homeowners however will own an extension ladder capable of reaching the gutters and eaves of a two-storey home. An 8 m extension ladder may seem expensive but the savings that you can make by doing the work yourself could justify the investment, and it will then be freely available for future maintenance work.

For one weekend's work you may prefer to hire the ladders from your local builders' merchant. You will find them in the Yellow Pages, and most will deliver and pick up equipment for a reasonable charge. Remember that the weekly hire charges often work out to be about 25 per cent of the cost of the equipment, so for that longer project, hiring may not be the most economical option.

A dual-purpose ladder which forms steps or extends is very handy to have. Attach-ments include stabilisers, a foot rest, ladder tray and ladder stay.

A ladder stay is a useful accessory. It clips to the rungs of the ladder and holds it away from the wall so that the ladder can be extended to a safe height for painting gutt-ering without resting on it.

One way to obtain these more expensive items of equip-ment is to share the cost with another member of your family or a neighbour.

Scaffold tower

For those jobs where conven-tional access is impossible, it may be necessary to hire a scaffold tower. Scaffold frames and planking may be obtained from any builders' merchant and can be safely erected by the average handyperson. Don't be intimidated by the thought. Two people can set up a 4 m tower in about 15 minutes. If possible, attach the tower to the house for extra stability. When erecting, or climbing up the tower, always climb up the inside. The tower must be vertical, so take time to adjust the feet properly (put a plank or paving slab under each foot for extra support on soft ground). A stepladder and bridging plank can be used with the tower to form an extension.

For most domestic projects, six 1800 x 1200 mm frames, adjustable legs and planking should be sufficient.

The scaffold can be erected in one position, sealer and undercoat applied on success-ive days and the scaffold moved to a different location and so on until completion.

The advantage of a scaffold tower is that you get a working platform at a useful height from which you will be able to paint all surfaces at the same time – gutters, eaves, fascias and downpipes, for example.

Making plans

Repainting the whole of a home is a daunting task. However, almost anyone can approach the job with confidence if they follow a few simple rules and work systematically.

With the cost of trades-people escalating rapidly, quotations for painting a reasonable-size home can vary considerably, ranging from suspiciously cheap to excessively high! An enthusi-astic amateur can do the same job for the cost of the materials over a month of weekends. A complete house-painting project will comprise the gutters, downpipes, eaves, walls and metalwork and windows, and any other exterior timber such as pergolas, doors, gates and the like. Certain general guide-lines apply for all of these.

Start from the top

❏ Gutters, fascias and eaves should be painted first. Then you should work from the top down, starting with walls and finishing off with the final coats to windows, doors and any detail work.

❏ Save the finer work until last. There is no advantage in completing window frames and the like first as paint will drip and spatter on the finish from gutters, eaves and walls and you may need to repaint.

❏ Try to plan the job in such

TIPSTRIP

CHEAP PAINTS AND GOOD PAINTS

Cheap paints are often a false economy. Cheap paint may be half the cost of a 'name brand', but inferior coverage and reduced service life can often cancel out the perceived savings.

a way that you won't need to lean a ladder against any freshly painted final coats. Why make more work?

All about paint

Paint may be expected to cover a multitude of sins, but ultimately the imperfections below will show through as the paint dries and cures.

Colour

As your home is your most valuable asset, choose the colour scheme carefully. The colours you choose will determine your home's outward appearance, both to visitors and prospective buyers.

Think carefully about how the colour scheme will work, and don't choose colours that are too radical – 'fashion' colours often won't last the distance and are costly to change.

Testing colours

Some paint companies have introduced small tins of paint for use as samples. When you test a colour on the walls of your home, make sure that you try the colour patch over a primed and undercoated area as paints appear different on different surfaces. The final colours will not be accurate samples if you test them on bare walls.

Test colours on all four walls of your home. Colour responds to reflected light

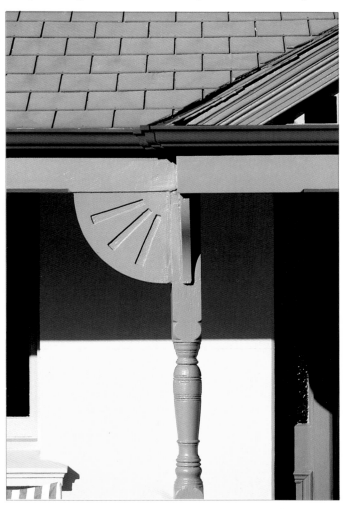

Decorative pattern and texture on an exterior

and a colour that is perfect on a western wall may not be so good on a southern wall if the light conditions are different.

Be aware that paints are generally darker when first applied and as they dry or cure the colour will fade slightly. On the other hand, paints look lighter on the manufacturer's colour card than they do when applied to the walls. Carefully checking the selected colours before you buy the final large batch could save a colour card disaster. We have all seen those houses where the colour choice was extreme, or the combination of colours distasteful – perhaps this could have been avoided if the owners had seen the right colours on the wall.

Oil-based or water-based paints?

Water-based paints are also known under the chemical term 'acrylics'. Acrylic paints may now be used as an alternative to most of the more traditional oil-based or solvent-based paints, and they have a number of significant advantages.

Acrylic paints may be applied directly over brick, concrete and render, without sealers or undercoats. They may be applied over reasonably fresh render and masonry, while oil-based paints have to be applied over dry surfaces. Acrylic paints may be applied over render that has cured for as little as four weeks. Oil-based paints must be applied over dry and fully cured surfaces and this may require at least six weeks for new render or brickwork.

A two-coat system using acrylic paint will adequately cover and protect masonry

TIPSTRIP

SHOP AROUND
Specialist trade suppliers are often prepared to supply the home owner and often offer paint at discount prices. Savings of as much as 50 per cent can be achieved by shopping around. Check the Yellow Pages for paint suppliers. It is also worth looking at the classified advertisements in the daily press and in DIY magazines.

Buy paint in the largest containers possible. Five 1 litre tins will cost about 25 per cent more than one 5 litre tin. General-purpose sealers and undercoats may be used for many purposes around the home and it is sensible to purchase these paints in the largest sizes available. Exterior paints will also be most economical when purchased in bulk containers.

The big advantage of buying colour-mixed final coats all at the same time is that the colour will be consistent through the whole batch. If your paint supplier makes a mistake in one of several smaller tins when the paint is mixed, the different colours will show up on the walls! Always buy a little more paint than the job requires so that repairs can be carried out if required at a later stage.

and render. Acrylic sealers may be used in extreme exposure conditions for additional protection. Oil-based paints generally require a three-coat system: sealer, and two topcoats.

Acrylic paints may provide superior service life compared to oil-based gloss paints due to their greater flexibility.

Cleaning up is easier with water-based paints and they are generally more environmentally friendly. Brushes and rollers will be easier to clean and will last much longer with acrylic paints.

How much paint?

Most paint companies provide coverage estimates on their published data sheets and on the tins of paint. These estimates are fairly accurate, but depend on variables such as the way you paint, the absorption of the material being painted, and the temperature of the surface and drying conditions. A roller will use more paint than a brush.

The cost of the paint itself is a small proportion of the value of the total job. A two-storey home of, say, 250 sq m of floor area will require something like the following paints:

40 litres stabilising solution
80 litres masonry paint (for two coats)
2.5 litres galvanised iron primer (gutters and down-pipes)
2.5 litres undercoat (gutters and downpipes)
5 litres gloss – enough for two coats (gutters and downpipes)
5 litres wood primer (doors, windows, eaves, fascias)
5 litres undercoat (doors, windows, eaves, fascias)
10 litres gloss – enough for two coats (doors, windows, eaves, fascias)
Plus cost of sandpaper; turps (white spirit); rolling equipment and brushes; hiring ladders, etc.

Naturally these figures will depend on many factors, like the number of windows and doors, and are given as a guide only.

Considering that the cost of materials may be as little as 10 per cent of the cost of a professional's quotation, considerable savings can be made by doing the job yourself.

The difference between using cheap low-quality paints and a premium brand will be insignificant when compared to the cost of the type of job described. Considering the enormous amount of labour involved in a major painting job, premium grade paint is worth the additional cost.

Preparation

Your project will only be as good as the preparation. A painting job, big or small, done over an inadequately prepared surface will neither last as long nor look as good as one done properly.

Paint is too expensive to be wasted – all surfaces to be painted should be dry and free of dust, with all surface roughness and imperfections attended to. Nails and screws should be fixed well below the surface of the material. Any holes need to be filled with the appropriate fillers and sanded smooth before you start painting.

If you are using water-based paint, this is especially important. The water in the paint can rust the unprotected steel and you will get spotting and rust staining. If you choose to use water-based paints externally, a good tip is to spot-prime the nail holes with an oil-based primer or undercoat before proceeding.

Old timber – painted

All loose paint should be removed by sanding or scraping, or with a blowtorch. For small areas and close to glass, chemical paint removers may be useful. As a rule of thumb, if the previous coats of old paint are sound and difficult to remove, they should probably not be disturbed.

A good trick is to cut the surface with a sharp knife and stick some masking tape over the cut. If the paint comes off when you remove the tape, it should be stripped.

Provide a 'key' for future coats of paint by lightly sanding the whole surface. This is especially important if the previous coats were a

Exterior wall surface

gloss finish. Sand the surface until it has a matt appearance. If you leave sections still glossy then the new paint may start peeling from that point.

One coat of undercoat and two topcoats of the chosen finish will be required if you are significantly changing the colour. One finish coat will generally be sufficient if you are simply repainting with a similar colour.

Dulux

House exterior

New timber – paint finishes

Punch all nails well below the surface and fill the holes with waterproof fillers. Any knots should be sealed with shellac knotting compound; any faults in the surface of the timber should be filled also.

All new timber should be primed with one coat of the appropriate wood primer. If you are using a water-based system it is advisable to spot-prime the nail heads and holes with an oil-based paint. Acrylic paints are the best choice for new timber because they have the flexibility to expand and contract with the timber and they allow moisture to 'breathe' out from the wood.

A light sanding between coats will remove dust particles and minor blemishes. Most timber will require two final coats of exterior paint.

New timber – clear or stain finishes

Some commercial timber windows come with a waxy protective coating. This is designed to reduce staining

from cement and concrete during building operations and may be removed with a rag soaked in turps (white spirit).

In unprotected timber, black unsightly stains can be caused by concrete and mortar spatters and by the rusting of fixings. It is essential that any concrete be removed immediately.

Some window manufacturers use staples to fix beads and other sections of the frames but neglect to fill the holes. This should be done as soon as the windows are delivered to avoid staining caused by rust.

All nail holes and defects in the timber must be filled with wood grain filler. It is recommended that you stain the fillers with the final topcoat stain. Fillers take stain differently when they are dry, and the filling can be conspicuous if this procedure is not followed. There are commercial wood fillers designed to match timber grain and stains and the correct grade and colour should be selected to match the type and colour of the timber. Knots should be

sealed with bleached shellac knotting compound.

If timber has been allowed to stand in the sun for any length of time, sections of the timber will have weathered and will take the stain inconsistently. Therefore it is good practice to stain-finish the timber as soon as possible after installation. If this is not possible, then a light sanding before staining is recommended.

If at all possible, where windows and exposed timbers are to be installed in inaccessible places, consideration should be given to stain-finishing the timber on the ground prior to installation. If access for future repainting is going to be difficult, extreme care should be taken in preparation of the surfaces – only the best quality materials should be used.

There are two types of 'transparent' finish which may be used on natural timber. Traditional varnishes and the more modern high-performance equivalents give limited protection to new timber and must be recoated every 2-4 years. Exterior stains are also available, and come in a range of colours. The deeper colours give greater protection to the timber. Polyurethane varnishes are not suitable for outdoor use as they break down under ultraviolet rays in sunlight. When this happens, sections of the timber will be exposed to the elements and the timber will weather. This normally causes the timber to lose its natural colour and turn grey. To restore it, the entire surface must be scraped back to remove the finish and a new timber surface exposed – this can be tedious and is often not very satisfactory.

When applying varnishes, use a new brush and rub down lightly between coats to remove any dust and blemishes. A nylon pan-scourer is

ideal for this since it will not damage the previous coat.

Stain finishes, on the other hand, penetrate into the timber and may be recoated without undue difficulty. A light sanding is all that should be required. Stain finishes will fade with time, and after several recoatings the colour may get darker.

Wood stains can be applied by brush, pad or rags. Stains are quite aggressive and protective gloves are essential. Drop sheets and protection of surrounding surfaces is also necessary because stains tend to drip and spatter. If applying stains with a brush, keep plenty of clean rags close by and rub off any excess stain, changing rags frequently. On completion of work the whole of the stained surface should be rubbed down with a lint-free rag to ensure penetration into the surface and to remove brushmarks.

Sealing

The right stuff

SURFACE	PREPARATION	TREATMENT
New brickwork	Point up mortar joints if required	Exterior acrylic sealer applied with brush or long nap roller on very exposed walls
	Ensure that the surface is completely dry	
	Remove all loose material by brushing with a wire brush	
	Stubborn mortar spatters may be removed with muriatic acid – protective goggles and clothes are essential when using acid cleaners	Two coats of exterior acrylic (or masonry paint) applied as above. Allow 24 hours drying time between coats for best results
Existing brickwork	Wash down walls with detergent to remove grime and rinse well	Spot-prime areas with acrylic sealer where removal of paint has exposed the brickwork
	Remove loose and peeling paint with a wire or stiff bristle brush	
	Allow adequate drying time	Apply two coats of exterior acrylic (or masonry paint) allowing 24 hours between coats
	Prepare as above	
New timber	Punch all nails well below the surface and fill with exterior filler. Seal knots with shellac knotting and fill surface defects	Apply acrylic timber primer to all exposed surfaces. If possible, prime the timber before construction
	Lightly sand with fine glasspaper to remove surface imperfections and to feather fillers to the timber surface	Apply two coats of acrylic low sheen gloss paint. Sand lightly between coats
Old timber with sound existing paint – especially doors and windows	Sand whole of surface with fine glasspaper to remove all traces of gloss and to provide a 'key' for future paint	Undercoat over repaired sections, and whole of surface if changing colour from dark shade to lighter
		One or two coats of exterior gloss or low sheen depending on coverage
	Fill any defects with exterior filler and spot-prime with acrylic primer or undercoat	In general, it is best to repaint timber that has been painted with oil-based paints with the same type of paint
Old timber with peeling or badly damaged paint	Remove all blistered and peeling paint by scraper, blowtorch or hot air gun. All paint should be removed to the bare timber	Prime and finish as for new timber
	Fill all cracks, holes and other defects with exterior fillers and sand smooth. Seal cracks between timber frames and masonry with non-hardening mastic	
Timber pergolas, fences, outdoor furniture, etc	Fill cracks and defects with exterior filler	Exterior acrylic treatments, such as Dulux Timbercolor, or 'Ranch'-style paints may be used directly over sound timber. One or two coats are required depending on the colour selected and the coverage

SURFACE	PREPARATION	TREATMENT
Stain-finished timber	Wipe down with turps (white spirit) to remove protective coatings if required. Fill nail holes and defects with wood filler, colour-matched to the final finishing colour. Sand lightly	Apply stain finishes with brush or by wiping with a soaked (but not saturated) rag. Wipe down with a lint-free rag on completion to remove excess stain and to encourage penetration into the timber
Timber with clear finishes or varnish	As for stain finishes. Take care to colour-match any fillers used to the colour of the timber	Use only a brand new brush to apply varnishes and clear finishes. Two coats are required, with light sanding between coats to remove dust spots and brushmarks
Timber with old clear finishes or varnish	Old varnish and badly deteriorated clear finishes should be completely removed. Paint strippers work well with varnish, but polyurethane finishes will need to be removed by scraping or sanding	Finish for new timber as above
New steel and galvanised iron	Remove all mortar spots and cement stains prior to painting	Prime with specially formulated galvanised iron primer
	Clean down with turps (white spirit) to remove grease and oil from manufacturing process	
	Wash down with detergent and water to remove all traces of turps (white spirit), etc and allow to dry	Undercoat with general-purpose undercoat and apply two coats of exterior gloss paint
Old painted metal surfaces and rusted metal	Sound paint over metal surfaces may be prepared with light sanding to remove all traces of gloss and to provide a key	Use cold galvanising paint to treat repaired sections where old galvanising has been damaged
	Remove all rust with a scraper and clean off with a wire brush	
	Apply a 'rust converter' over all damaged sections	Undercoat repaired sections with an acrylic undercoat. Apply two coats of exterior gloss paint
	Rusted metal gutters are best replaced	
Non-galvanised steel	Clean down with turps (white spirit) to remove grease and oil from manufacture	Prime with red oxide or zinc phosphate primer, undercoat with general-purpose undercoat and apply two coats of the selected finish
	Remove all rust with a scraper and clean off with a wire brush	
	Apply a 'rust converter' over all damaged sections	
Aluminium and copper	Clean down as for galvanised steel, remove all corroded or tarnished surfaces with a non-metallic scouring pad	Use phosphate-based primers and finish as for galvanised steel
Plastic downpipes and gutters	These materials normally do not require painting, however if necessary they may be treated as for galvanised steel	Use acrylic primers or undercoat and finish with two coats of selected exterior finish

Brickwork, blockwork and rendered surfaces

Oil-based finish

New brickwork should be left for six months after construction to ensure that any moisture has dried out and that all efflorescence has ceased. There is no point in painting wet brickwork as the paint will flake off or peel in a short time.

Leave mortar and rendered masonry until it has comprehensively dried out. The walls should preferably be painted in summer when the drying conditions are better. If the mortar joints show through the render, it indicates that the wall is still too wet for paint to be applied.

Apply masonry paint directly to brickwork or render. You won't need sealer unless the surface of masonry is powdery/friable. If necessary, seal masonry walls first with a high quality acrylic sealer. Due to the rough surfaces, application by long nap roller is recommended. Work the sealer well into the surface and apply as generously as possible. Undercoat with a general-purpose exterior undercoat if a high-gloss finish is desired, and finish with one or two topcoats.

> **TRICKS OF THE TRADE**
> Use a 75 mm nail to punch four equally spaced holes in the lip of a paint tin. When you are painting from the tin the paint which collects in the lip will drip down into the tin rather than down the outside. Better still, buy a paint kettle.

Acrylic (water-based)

Acrylic paints may be applied over new render and masonry with shorter drying and curing times than oil-based systems require. At least four weeks should be allowed for new render to cure properly, but this time should be extended where possible if the drying conditions are not satisfactory. New brickwork may be painted after fourteen days, again depending on the drying conditions.

Water-based paints should be applied over an acrylic sealer and two final coats of good quality exterior acrylic but it is common practice to neglect the sealer and use two coats of exterior acrylic paint.

Pergolas and other garden structures

The best time to paint a pergola is when the timber is on the ground before it is erected. This is good advice but unfortunately is rarely followed.

Exterior timber, particularly rough-sawn timber, may be finished with special exterior acrylic timber paints, e.g 'Ranch' paints, designed for the purpose. These paints can be applied without primers and undercoats, and the lighter colours are dense enough to be applied as a single-coat system. The Dulux Timbercolor range is also made for the purpose – it contains pigments to prevent discoloration and fading, and is flexible enough to move with the timber. It is also harmless to plants and animals when dry.

Trellising and latticework, increasingly popular in modern homes, are best painted with spray-painting equipment. Painting latticework with a brush is time-consuming and tedious. Airless spray guns are quite economical and can complete the job in half the time. Spray guns may be hired if you only want to do this job once.

Metal gutters and downpipes

Most metal downpipes are made from galvanised steel. When this metal is new, it will be oily from the manufacturing process and should not be painted until the metal has weathered or been carefully cleaned. Many new homes

House with painted brickwork

Dulux

suffer the problem of paint peeling from metal gutters and downpipes because they were painted too soon after installation.

Special galvanised iron primers are available for preparation. Some are water-based acrylic-type paints and some are the more traditional oil-based etch primers. Both types are satisfactory for galvanised iron, with the caution that the water-based paints do not adhere well to silicone sealants, which are universally used for caulking. If you have too much silicone

GREEN TIP
Never clean up water-based or oil-based paints in the sink. Clean water-based paints with the garden hose on waste ground and allow the contaminated water to filter through the ground. It is not advisable to do this on ground used for growing plants.

Oil-based paints should be cleaned up with turps (white spirit) or special brush-cleaning compounds and the waste stored in containers to allow the solids to settle. The turps (white spirit) may then be filtered and re-used, and the solids disposed of in the rubbish.

Grey and mushroom-coloured latticework on a balcony screens off neighbouring property from view

Skill Class
Painting gutters and downpipes

Repainting gutters is one job that could be completed in a weekend and it will really improve the appearance of your home. Unfortunately, many builders paint metal gutters too soon after they have been installed and the paint tends to peel off. The only solution is to remove all of the peeling or flaking paint. Scraping or sanding should be avoided as it may damage the protective galvanised surfaces.

Peeling paint can be removed with paint strippers or with the sparing use of a blowtorch or electric hot air gun. Take extreme care not to overheat the metal. Then clean the whole of the metal with turps (white spirit) to remove residual paint.

Protect surfaces with drop sheets and mask off windows and door openings to prevent paint spatters.

Reprime the gutters, after cleaning, with a special-purpose galvanised iron primer.

Work off a ladder supported off the walls if at all possible so that it does not damage the fresh coats of paint. Work from right to left if you are right-handed, going around the house in a clockwise direction. The reverse applies for left-handed painters.

Use a paint kettle attached to your ladder and only fill it to a level of about 75 mm maximum. Avoid working from the tins in which the paint is supplied, to avoid drips and spillages and to prevent the paint from thickening.

The topcoats should be acrylic or high-gloss. A very light sanding between coats is needed to remove dust and blemishes for a first-class job.

sealant smeared over the metal, it may be better to use the oil-based type of primer.

Once the metal has been primed, finishing will consist of two topcoats.

As a general comment, if you are using oil-based primers, it is better to use oil-based undercoats and topcoats to keep the paint types consistent.

TRICKS OF THE TRADE
Most paints come ready for use and will not require thinning. Old paints which have dried out may require a little thinning to improve workability. Check the instructions on the tin for the correct thinning agent. Normally, turps (white spirit) or paint thinners are recommended for oil-based paints and water for acrylic paints.

Use thinners sparingly and stir the paint thoroughly. It's always better to add thinners a little at a time, rather than adding too much initially.

Non-drip paints will lose this property if they are thinned and stirred.

Painting roofs

When winter wind and rain come in through the holes in your galvanised iron roof, you know it's time to take drastic action! But you may not need to re-roof. Consider repairing the holes and treating your weatherworn covering. The metal may be rusty but still basically sound, in which case it can be restored with a rust converter – a paint-on product that turns rust back into solid metal. If your corrugated iron has lost much of its protective galvanising, it can be treated with an inhibitor that will prevent rust.

Rust
Dealing with rust will be one of your first priorities.

❑ Remove all loose rust, powder and dirt with a wire brush

❑ Remove oil and grease with turps (white spirit)

❑ Apply rust converter only to rusted but essentially sound areas

❑ Treat areas that are not badly rusted with a rust inhibitor (allow 24 hours for anti-rust solutions to dry out)

❑ Ensure the surface of the roof is in a condition to give good adhesion (follow the manufacturer's recommendations)

Most paints recommended for old roofs are oil-based, many of which contain rust-inhibiting chemicals. A primer may be needed for the whole surface of the roof, although some manufacturers would recommend a red oxide primer only for rust-treated areas. Priming is very important as the primer has qualities that enable it to stick to a galvanised surface.

Allow 24 hours between coats, unless instructed otherwise by the manufacturer.

The easiest way to paint a roof is with a long-handled roller made of plastic foam, shaped to fit two or three corrugations.

A new metal roof should be left for six months before being painted to create a

Dulux

Painted metal roof

surface that will give maximum paint adhesion. The roof should be thoroughly cleaned before painting – by washing down with turps (white spirit). If you intend using water-based paints, wash down the surface with soapy water and rinse well. Once you choose a particular paint system, you must follow the manufacturer's instructions.

Skill Class
Painting timber windows

Painting timber in an old home can be a very satisfying home improvement project and nothing dresses up a home better than neatly painted windows.

Timber windows are often repainted in such a way that the paint has caused the sashes or casements to jam. If this is the case, you will probably have to partially dismantle the window, remove the excess paint and repaint from scratch.

Before you start painting however, check the condition of the windows and complete any required repairs. Check that the sash cords are in good condition as their replacement at a later stage will damage the paint. Replace any badly rusted or worn hinges. Check the condition of timber beads, storm moulds and the weather-proofing and replace any rotted or damaged timber.

Remove excess and peeling paint with a paint remover, scraper or by blowtorch or hot air gun. Take care not to over-heat the glass or to damage the timber by burning or by gouging with the scraper. After all the paint has been removed, lightly sand the timber, fill any holes, knots or

TRICKS OF THE TRADE
While masking off windows may seem a waste of time, it saves cleaning up the glass on completion. Use masking tape and newspaper to mask both the glass and the window frames. Remember to remove the masking immediately after the paint is dry. If masking tape is left out in the sun for a few days it will become impossible to remove!

imperfections with exterior filler, replace any cracked putty and prime with wood primer. Complete the job with one coat of undercoat and one or two coats of topcoat. Two light coats of paint are better than one thick one. Sanding lightly between coats of paint will leave a smooth and defect-free surface. Take the paint about 3 mm on to the glass to make a seal.

Insert small nails in the grooves of sash windows to keep the parts separate while the paint dries, and ensure that the sashes will not stick in position. Alternatively, move the sashes up and down several times as the paint dries.

Repainting your front door

Your front door is a very visible part of your home and will receive close inspection, so take the time to do a first-class job. Doors, particularly entry doors, get a lot of use and any bumps and scratches will stand out.

Preparation should commence with the careful removal of door handles, numbers, bell pushes and the like as these items are difficult to mask off with masking tape and can be permanently damaged by sanding.

Check the fit of your door to ensure that there is enough room for additional thicknesses of paint. If your door is a tight fit, it may be necessary to sand back the door jambs, and prime and undercoat again.

If your door has been finished previously with a gloss (enamel) paint, sand it lightly all over to remove any traces of shine and to provide a key for future coats of paint.

Fill any dents, defects and scratches with wood filler. Make sure the filler has completely dried (usually overnight) before you sand it smooth. For major dents in edges and corners of doors where heavy wear occurs, epoxy-based two-part fillers can also be used. Spot-prime any repaired areas with undercoat or primer. Feather back repaired sections to blend in with the undisturbed surface. Use fine glasspaper or wet-and-dry paper for a really smooth finish.

Mask off hinges with masking tape using a trimming knife to ensure a good fit. It's next to impossible to paint around hinges without getting some paint on them – excessive paint will cause hinges to stick and make closing the doors difficult. It is best to avoid the problem by careful masking.

After preparation and final sanding is complete, clean up the work area and remove all dust. If you have pets, keep them away until the paint is dry! Clean down the surface with a rag dampened with turps (white spirit) and allow the door to completely dry before painting.

Gloss paints can be tricky and they are prone to sags and wrinkling if applied too thickly. Two thin coats are always better than one thick coat.

Apply gloss paints in sections, working from the top of the door to the bottom. Work the brush horizontally while laying the paint on and use vertical strokes to blend in the sections. Paint in 300 mm to 450 mm horizontal bands

Painting a timber fence

A dilapidated fence with peeling paint is scarcely the right welcome to your home! Painting the fence is a rewarding home improvement project and can provide a much needed lift to your home's appearance.

Whether you are painting a new fence or repairing an existing timber fence, the project can seem quite daunting. A picket fence or one constructed from latticework or trellising is very time-consuming to paint with a brush and impossible to paint with a roller!

The easiest solution is often an electric spray-painting kit. It will give the best results and can reduce the time required to a bare minimum. This simple piece of painting equipment can be hired from your local builders' merchant.

When spray painting, consideration must be given to masking off precious plants, paving and other surrounding materials. Detach any plants, creepers and vines which may be supported by the fence and cover them with drop sheets to prevent paint spatters damaging foliage. Never use spray-painting equipment in strong winds.

across the door, taking particular care not to leave a bead of paint on the edges.

Lay off the whole of the surface with vertical strokes to leave a consistent pattern of brushmarks. Check to see if there are any runs or sags and remove them with a nearly dry brush.

Sand lightly between coats to remove dust spots and brushmarks.

Traditional paint finishes for timber fences are gradually being replaced by modern acrylic paints, which are designed to be applied directly to bare timber. They may also be applied over existing sound paint after sanding the surfaces with medium glasspaper.

Two basic painting systems may be used for painting and repainting timber fences. Conventional systems, comprising a primer, undercoat and two topcoats, can be very labour intensive, and the area of fence can be quite daunting. Acrylic timber paints can be applied directly and are a good alternative to stain finishes as they are less messy to apply and give an excellent service life – some are capable of covering in one coat, greatly reducing the labour required.

The procedure adopted for repainting a timber fence is the same as for all external timberwork.

❑ First, all loose, damaged and flaking paint must be removed by scraping and the bare surfaces properly prepared. Thick build-ups of paint are best removed with a blow torch or hot air gun.

❑ Any spots of bare timber where the old primers have been removed should be reprimed with exterior wood primer. The existing sound paint should be lightly sanded to provide a key for future coats.

❑ Two coats of exterior acrylic will complete the job.

❑ For rejuvenating clear stain finishes the whole of the surface should be lightly sanded and the stain applied by brush, spray or stain-soaked rags. Always wear protective rubber gloves and long-sleeved clothing when applying stains as they are difficult to remove.

Two-colour picket fence

GLOSSARY

Anti-fungicide: A solution applied to walls where mildew or mould is a problem. Anti-fungicide has a fairly short life. If you need to treat your walls be sure to start wallpapering soon after.

Antiquing: The process of creating the appearance of mellowness, age and use.

Architrave: The moulding around a doorway or window opening.

Bolt: A roll of wallpaper as it's supplied by the manufacturer. A standard bolt or roll is 10.05 m long and 520 mm wide (11 yd x 21 in).

Batch number: A number stamped on every roll which indicates the batch or printing job lot. Because printing processes may vary, it's important to make sure all the rolls you buy carry the same batch number.

Borders: Narrow strips of wallpaper, easy to apply and with unlimited decorative possibilities.

Bubbles: These are often caused by paste and sometimes appear beneath the wallpaper as soon as it has been hung. They usually dry out. If the bubble is trapped air, use a syringe to inject paste beneath the paper then smooth out.

Butt joints: Strips of wallpaper matched and hung alongside each other edge to edge so the joins don't overlap.

Chair rail: The moulding or rail fixed to a wall at chair height.

Companions: Different wallcoverings designed and coloured to relate with each other.

Cornice: Usually a plaster moulding separating walls from ceiling.

Crackle medium: A decorative paint finish that looks like cracked and split paint (see page 46).

Dado: The lower part of the wall, often to chair height, which may be defined by a moulding or border.

DPC: Damp-proof course.

Dragging: A decorative paint technique whereby a dragging brush is dragged through a glaze to produce a brushed, textured effect (see page 44).

Drop pattern: A wallpaper pattern which repeats itself diagonally.

Embossed paper: Sometimes known as Duplex, this is wallpaper with a raised pattern or relief effect. Don't use a roller when smoothing or you risk flattening the embossing!

Fixtures: Refers to lights, switch plates and other permanent items attached to walls.

Florals: Wallpapers with designs consisting mainly of flowers and foliage.

Frieze: See Borders.

Glaze: A semi-translucent coat of paint painted onto an opaque background.

Glue size: Applied to walls before papering, it allows you to move or 'slip' the wallpaper into position and creates better adhesion.

Lining paper: Plain wallpaper used as a base to provide a smooth surface for paper hanging, especially on uneven walls.

Machine printing: Most wallpapers today are manufactured on a rotary type printing press which produces consistent and clear patterns.

Marbling: A decorative paint finish that imitates the vein-type pattern in marble (see page 47).

Matching: Hanging strips of paper so the pattern will be in correct relation to the previous strip.

Mineral turpentine (white spirit): A colourless flammable liquid – an essential oil – containing a mixture of terpenes; used as a solvent for paints. Also known as turps.

Painted finish: A paint finish applied to a surface to protect it; a finish applied to a surface to create contrast, texture or pattern, or to help an item blend with existing surroundings. Common techniques used to create a painted finish include stippling, sponging, dragging and marbling.

Parchment finish: Also called 'two-process ragging', this decorative paint finish requires two glazes and produces a highly textured finish and irregular areas of colour where the first glaze has soaked up the second glaze (see page 45).

Paste: Adhesive used to attach wallpaper to walls. Most common are cellulose and starch.

Pattern: The design on wallpaper which is repeated throughout the roll.

Peelable wallpaper: Wallpaper with a vinyl layer that allows it to be peeled off the wall without scraping. It leaves a thin layer of paper which can easily be removed or retained, if sound.

Picture rail: The moulding or rail near the top of a wall from which pictures can be hung.

Plumb line: Weight attached to a length of string and used to obtain the perpendicular for accurate paper hanging.

Polyurethane: A hard yet resilient transparent coating.

Pretrimmed wallpaper: Wallpaper from which the manufacturer has trimmed the edges.

Prepasted wallpaper: Most wallpaper today has a film of dry paste on the back which only requires wetting to gain adhesion.

Preparation: Preparing the wall or ceiling prior to hanging. An important step in paper hanging which may involve sanding down and sizing the surface.

Primary colours: Pure red, yellow and blue.

Renovation: Update from the original.

Reveal: Timber extension of a window frame to the interior.

Roll: See Batch.

Scrubbable wallpaper: Vinyl (polyvinyl chloride or PVC) wallpapers are usually scrubbable and can be cleaned using soap or detergent and a soft bristle brush.

Scumble medium: A translucent medium composed of linseed oil, turps (white spirit), whiting and extenders to create a longer drying time.

Sealer: A coating to provide a suitable surface for final coatings; a liquid used to seal porous surfaces such as plasterboard and plaster which might otherwise leach moisture from the paste and prevent adhesion.

Seams: There are several methods of joining seams. The butt joint in which the edges fit tightly together produces the smoother effect and is the most popular because it leaves a flat, invisible seam.

Secondary colours: Mixed from pure primary colours: green from yellow and blue; orange from red and yellow; violet from red and blue.

Shading: See Batch number.

Size: See Glue size.

Slip: The ability of wallpaper to be moved and patterns matched when in contact with the wall surface. The application of glue size to the wall before commencing papering further assists slip.

Sponging: A decorative paint technique whereby a glaze is applied using a sea sponge, and then a second sponge dipped in turps (white spirit) is used to create patterns in the glaze (see page 45).

Stippling: A decorative paint technique whereby dots or flecks of paint are applied with a stipple brush (see page 44).

Stopping compound: A filler or putty for filling blemishes in timbers.

Straightedge: A ruler used to give a clean and consistent edge when cutting or trimming wallpaper.

Straight match: Patterned wallpaper where the design is such that the matching points on either side of a strip are opposite each other.

Strippable wallpaper: Wallpaper that can be completely removed without scraping.

Substrate: The backing of wallpaper which is laminated to the design layer.

Sugar soap: Coarse abrasive soap used to thoroughly clean, degrease and prepare walls for paper hanging.

Trompe l'oeil finish: A painted or decorated effect which gives an illusion of reality by 'imitating' the real thing.

Turps: See Mineral turpentine (white spirit).

Vinyl: A range of durable wallpapers which include flexible film, resin and plastic coating.

Water trough: The shallow box used when hanging prepasted wallpaper.

CONVERSION TABLE

Although most people have some working knowledge of metrics, many cannot visualise the actual size of a metric measurement. Hopefully the following table will help.

LENGTH
1 mm approx $3/64$ inch
10 mm approx $3/8$ inch (a mortar joint, thickness of the average little finger)
25 mm approx 1 inch (everyone knows what an inch is!)
230 mm approx 9 inches (1 brick)
820 mm approx 32 inches (an average door width)
2400 mm approx 8 feet (10 bonded bricks, or minimum ceiling height)
1 m approx 39 inches
1.8 m approx 6 feet (a tall male)
2.04 m – just under 7 feet (the height of the average door)
3 m approx 10 feet

VOLUME
1 litre approx 1.8 pints (a carton of milk)
4.5 litres approx 1 gallon (a large paint tin)

AREA
1 sq m approx 1 sq yd
9.3 sq m approx 1 building square – 100 sq ft

INDEX

ACKNOWLEDGMENTS

The publisher wishes to thank the following for their assistance in the production of this book. Apologies to any individuals or companies not specifically mentioned.

The Australian Wallpaper Council – and in particular, Doug Stuckey of Vision Wallcoverings; Laura Ashley; Forbo/Nairn Decor; and Wilson Wallcoverings – for providing pictorial references, materials for photography and technical advice.

Dulux, Australia, for their technical advice and assistance in providing photographs, tools and paint for photography.

Jennifer Bennell and her team at The Painted Finish for their help and expertise in the area of decorative paint techniques.

Virginia Carroll, interior designer and colour consultant, for her assistance in providing locations and colour analysis.

The publisher also wishes to give special thanks to the following companies, who provided materials for photography or in some other way contributed to this book.

Tempo Interiors and Wardlaw for supplying selected fabrics and wallpapers for photography (p.12, lower right; pp.14-15; and pp.16-17) and for supplying wallpapers pictured on p.26.

Wattyl for 'Before' photograph of whitewood chest (p.43).

Clarke & Walker, Mitre 10, for supplying tools and equipment for photography.

The Balmain Garden Centre for plants (pictured on pp.66-67).